Hawaii Cooks
Throughout the Year

By Maili Yardley

Paintings By
Paul T. Yardley

Published by Editions Limited

Published by Editions Limited
111 Royal Circle
Honolulu, Hawaii 96816

Copyright © 1990 by Maili Yardley

Book Design by Cindy Turner, Turner & de Vries

ISBN 0-915013-13-4

First Edition 1990
Printed in Hong Kong

TABLE OF CONTENTS

◆

This book is fondly dedicated to my girls...
Laura, Louli, Cynthia, Marci, Norma, Gay, and Melinda,
All Good Cooks In Their Own Kitchens!

PREFACE

◆

This book is the result of the urging of family, friends, and loyal readers of "The Island Way", my column published weekly in the Honolulu Advertiser, to do "just one more!" I am, indeed, grateful for your encouragement and kokua.

Instead of following the usual pattern of listing recipes under catagories, I've followed a whim and encompassed the contents in twelve chapters according to the month, focusing on seasons, holidays, and occasions.

Since this is my fourth cookbook, I've done something I've always wanted to do! In February you'll find Valentine's Day and all the "sweets for the sweet" in tempting desserts. Since Easter usually comes in April, you'll find appropriate recipes there. Guess where you'll find help for Thanksgiving and Christmas!

Hapa-Haole in flavor, you'll find bits of Island lore and information on our foods, such as when fruits are in season and recipes especially for popular Island produce.

My sincere hope is that you will refer to this book often and enjoy using the many recipes from the columns plus a lot of the tried and true favorites over the years.

Hele Mai Ai!!!!

ABBREVIATIONS

C-	cup	ea-	each
hr-	hour	in-	inch
lb-	pound	min-	minute
oz-	ounce	pt-	pint
qt-	quart	S&P-	salt and pepper
t-	teaspoon	T-	tablespoon

YEAR-ROUND KITCHEN AIDS

To slice mushrooms easily, just place in egg slicer and presto!

When testing baked potatoes for doneness, always spear them with a toothpick. It lets out a minimum of steam.

Like your tomatoes peeled? Place fresh tomatoes in brown paper bag, make a cuff around the top, set in corner of sink, and pour in boiling water. Bag will split after few seconds...just long enough so the tomatoes will be ready to skin. Refrigerate in cellophane bag.

To release a glass stuck in another glass, pour a little oil between and wiggle gently apart.

Lemon is a fantastic cleansing agent. Rub it on your hands to remove garlic and onion odors. Add a bit of lemon juice to dishwater. It cuts grease and makes dishes sparkle.

Lemon juice keeps cut avocados, bananas, and apples from turning brown. Use in tangy salad dressings instead of vinegar.

Use the water from boiled eggs to water your house plants; it has good mineral content.

If wine or coffee is spilled on the carpet, quickly pour bottled soda water directly on spill and blot with paper towel. It really is a fantastic remedy, and especially good for doggie puddles!

Copy the following and tuck into a drawer near the stove, and you will find yourself referring to it quite frequently for flavoring.

ASPARAGUS: chives, caraway, lemon juice

GREEN BEANS: onion, paprika, mustard in butter, parsley, basil, dill, and lemon juice

BEETS: parsley, chives, cloves, lemon, horseradish, paprika, nutmeg, brown sugar or vinegar, and sugar

BROCCOLI: lemon juice, chives, caraway, marjoram, and oregano

BRUSSELS SPROUTS: lemon juice and onion

CABBAGE: caraway or poppy seed, parsley, tarragon, lemon juice, small amount dry mustard, or 1/2 t nutmeg to 1 C white sauce

CARROTS: parsley, chives, thyme, lemon juice, and mint

CAULIFLOWER: nutmeg, marjoram, parsley, and chives

ONIONS: dash of cloves and paprika

PEAS: parsley, thyme, chives, tarragon, and mint

POTATOES: chopped parsley, chives, and paprika

SQUASH: marjoram, basil, chives, nutmeg, curry, or cloves

SWEET POTATOES: brown sugar and nutmeg or orange juice and brown sugar, parsley, cloves, or cinnamon

TOMATOES: basil, parsley, onion, tarragon, and marjoram

The following are bottles you shouldn't be without on the shelf.

(If you use fresh herbs, triple the recipe when calling for dried herbs.)

CELERY SEED: enhances pickles, potato salad, coleslaw dressing, and tomato juice

SESAME SEED: used mostly in breads or rolls, some pastries, added to raw fish, noodles, and buttered vegetables.

DILL: used for pickles, sea food, and salads

MARJORAM: used mostly in tomato and egg dishes, meats, soups, and fowl stuffing

ROSEMARY: milder than sage and a good substitute for fowl stuffing, for pork and lamb, and especially spaghetti sauce

BAY LEAVES: an important flavoring for stews, soups, sea food chowders, gravies, and marinades. Remove before serving.

Besides these seasonings, a well stocked shelf should contain at all times: Curry Powder, Ground Ginger, Minced Onions, Garlic Puree, Beef and Chicken Bouillon Cubes, 5 Island Spice, Poultry Seasoning and Sage. Cinnamon and Nutmeg are two of the most frequently used spices. Keep Paprika bottle in the refrigerator.

The following herbs can be raised in individual pots to be available at all times.

BASIL: to toss in green salads or enhance stews, but always for any tomato dish.

FLAT LEAFED CHIVES: milder than garlic and onion, but adds a subtle flavor when chopped and added to salads, cream cheese, omelets, and as a garnish for soup.

PARSLEY: snip for garnish, chop for salads, stuffings, gravies, cream sauces, eggs, and sandwich fillings.

MINT: a must for iced tea and to use chopped in fruit compotes, sauce for lamb, garnish for drinks, fruit salads, and some vegetables

NOTES

Anna's Ranch   *Collection of the Artist*

JANUARY

*It's January, the calm after the
storm, and the beginning of a new year.
Anyone for resolutions!*

Twelfth Night, ending the period of Christmas festivities, falls on the 6th. According to a long-standing custom, it's time to take down the tree and return the house to normal.

After all the holiday feasts, maybe we should think of simpler meals and trying out some new dishes. Hot soups hit the spot when the weather turns coolish.

Familiarize yourself with the year-round Island fruits and vegetables, and include our available fresh produce in your daily menus. Throughout the year you can usually always depend on finding avocados, bananas, coconuts, and about now the Surinam Cherries.

NEW DISHES OR OLD FAVORITES

It's a New Year! Why not try out some new dishes! Change is good!

OXTAIL STEW

Make this the day before so you can discard the thick crust of fat that forms on top.

Dredge 4 lbs cut-up oxtail and 1-1/2 lbs lean stew meat in a bag containing flour, paprika, S&P to taste. Add sufficient oil to large pot and brown oxtail and stew meat a few at a time so as to brown evenly. Pour off grease, return meat to pot, and add 2 cans bouillon, and simmer for an hour. Add 4 cloves minced garlic, 3 large quartered onions, 2 sliced carrots, 1 bay leaf, 6 peppercorns, Worcestershire Sauce to taste, and simmer about 2 hrs or until meat is very tender. Add 1-1/2 C sherry and simmer about 15 mins. Thicken with leftover seasoned flour combined with some water, and serve hot.

LAMB KIDNEYS IN WINE SAUCE

Saute 9 lamb kidneys, sliced, and 1 t grated onion in 2-1/2 T butter for 5 mins. Sprinkle 2-1/2 T flour over them and stir. Add 1 C stock gradually, season with salt and paprika to taste. Remove from fire and add 2 T sherry. Serve over toast slices.

TONGUE

Wash fresh tongue and rinse well. Simmer in large pot with 1 C each of white wine, water, and beef broth, quartered onions, 2 bay leaves, 2 T pickling spices, dill seed, S&P, and 1 stalk chopped celery.

Simmer for 3 to 3-1/2 hrs or until tender. Cool, remove, and peel outer skin. Slice on bias and serve hot or cold. Or throw out water and return tongue to pot with 1 #303 can whole or stewed tomatoes, 2 T vinegar, 1 T brown sugar, S&P, and can of baby onions. Simmer to flavor and serve hot with horseradish.

ORIENTAL LIVER

Remove skin and membrane from 1 lb liver and cut in 1/2 inch strips. Marinate in following sauce: 5 T soy, 2 T sugar, 1 T sake or sherry, and 1/2 t grated ginger. When marinated, strain, and shake liver pieces in bag with 1/2 C flour to coat each piece. Fry in hot oil quickly on both sides until brown and crispy.

ANN LEE HARRIS' SWEETBREADS

Sweetbreads act as the thymus gland and are found in the neck of young animals, but disappear after maturity.

To prepare enough for 6, use approximately 3 lbs of sweetbreads. Simmer in water to cover, to which 1/4 C of vinegar has been added, for 15 mins. Plunge into ice water and let cool. Remove membrane and slice lengthwise into 1/2 in thick slices.

Either dip in melted butter, place on broiler rack and broil till lightly browned, S&P to taste, and serve on toast points. Or prepare a rich cream sauce, add sherry and cooked sweetbreads, chopped pimentos, 1 t minced onion, and some ground ham to enhance the flavor. Pour into casserole and bake to heat.

OSSO BUCCO

Saw 2-1/2 lbs of knuckle of veal into 2-in pieces, making sure marrow remains inside the bone. Chop up 2 carrots, 2 stalks celery, and stir into 2-1/2 T of butter until almost brown, then add 1/4 C chopped onions and the veal. Season well with S&P and stir to brown meat well. Add 1 t flour combined with 1 T butter, and continue cooking another 7 mins.

Stir in 1 C tomato paste alternately with 1/2 C dry white wine and 1/2 C hot veal stock or bouillon, to barely cover the meat. Add 2 strips lemon peel, 1 bay leaf, 2 T chopped parsley, and 1/2 t thyme. Bring to a boil, cover, and simmer gently for at least 1-1/2 hrs, stirring to avoid sticking. Place meat on platter and strain sauce over it with a sprinkling of grated lemon rind and chopped parsley.

PICKLED SPARE RIBS

Brown 4 lbs cut-up spare ribs, pour off fat, and add following mixture: 1/2 C each sugar, soy and vinegar, 3 cloves garlic, minced, finger of ginger, sliced, and simmer slowly for 1-1/2 to 2 hrs or until meat is tender and done.

VINEGAR ROAST PORK

Marinate a 4 to 5 lb pork roast for 2 to 3 days in following marinade: 1-1/2 C water, 3 large pieces garlic, 3 T salt, and 1 t pepper. Refrigerate. Roast pork in this liquid and allow 25 mins for each lb of meat. Add potatoes and carrots an hour before it is done. Serves 6.

FAMILY APPEASERS

PORK CHOP CASSEROLE

Brown 4 pork chops. Combine 1 can mushroom soup, 1/2 C sherry, dash of oregano, 2 T sugar, and 4 small quartered onions or can of small onions, drained. Pour evenly over chops in casserole. Bake 1-1/2 hrs in 350 oven.

Serve with **SPICED RED CABBAGE**

In glass pot combine 2-1/2 lbs shredded red cabbage, 1 red apple, peeled, cored and quartered, 1 finely chopped onion, 2 bay leaves, 1 t salt, and 1/2 C water. Cook, covered, over moderately high heat for 10 mins, stirring occasionally. Simmer for 15-20 mins or until cabbage is tender. Remove bay leaves, stir in 1/2 C sherry and 1/2 t cider vinegar. Add brown sugar to taste.

ANNE SEMINOLE'S POT ROAST IN BEER

Place a 3 to 4 lb pot roast, the cheapest you can find with bone in, in 9x13 in baking pan. Do not brown the meat first.

In a bowl, combine 1 12-oz can beer, 1/2 C brown sugar, 1 14-oz bottle of ketchup, 1/4 t ea seasoning salt and sweet basil, and blend. Pour the mixture over the meat and cover tightly with foil. Bake at 325 about 3 hrs or until tender.

SPICED POT ROAST

Use an eye or heel of round chuck.

Mix 1-1/2 C cider, 1 T brown sugar, 1/4 t ea cinnamon and ginger, and 2 whole cloves. Pour over 4 lb beef chuck, solid or rolled, cover, and let stand overnight in refrigerator.

Remove from marinade, wipe dry, dredge with flour, and season with S&P. Sear in 2 T oil in heavy kettle or Dutch oven till well browned. Add marinade, cover, and cook over low heat about 3 hrs or until meat is tender, turning frequently to cook uniformly. Thicken gravy, stirring in paste of 1 T ea flour and water and cooking about 3 mins.

Serve with buttered noddles.

FOIL ROAST OF BEEF is a cheaper cut made tender by long cooking and does save dish washing!

Mix together 1 package dried onion soup mix and 1 can cream of mushroom soup. Place a 3-4 lb chuck or rump roast (or stew meat) on heavy foil and pour soup over and around meat. Bring sides of foil together and fold over securely. Pull up short ends and securely fold to keep in steam. Place on baking sheet and roast about 4 hrs in 325 oven. Test for doneness the last hr. Meat should be tender.

Put baking potatoes in the oven last 1-1/2 hr.

Serve with **BEAN CASSEROLE** that can bake the last half hour.

In casserole layer the following: 2 boxes French-cut frozen string beans partially cooked, 1 package raw bean sprouts, 1 large can mushroom stems and pieces, 1 small can diced water chestnuts, chopped, and 1 can mushroom soup. Bake in 350 oven 1/2 hr. The last ten mins sprinkle canned French fried onions and grated sharp cheddar cheese over all and bake again.

POTATO AND FRANKFURTER CASSEROLE

In a frying pan cook 1/4 C chopped onion in 2 T oil until limp.

In a bowl mix 2 T flour, S&P to taste, 1 T sugar, 1 t dry mustard, 1/2 t celery seed, and blend thoroughly into onions. Add 2/3 C water and bring to boil.

Split 1 lb of franks lengthwise, cut twice crosswise. Arrange alternate layers of 4 C thinly sliced raw potatoes and franks in casserole, and pour the sauce over the top. Cover and bake at 375 50 mins or until potatoes are tender. Pour 2 T vinegar over, cover, and bake another 5 mins. Serves 6.

BARBECUED PORK AND BAKED BEANS

Pour 2 cans baked beans into casserole and even out. Arrange 6 lean pork chops on top. Combine 3 T prepared mustard, 1-1/2 T ea catsup, lemon juice, and brown sugar, 1/2 T salt, 1/4 t pepper, dash of Tabasco sauce, and spread over pork chops. Sprinkle evenly with 3/4 C chopped onion. Top it all with slices of lemon, and bake at 325 for 1-1/2 hrs. Serves 6.

GROUND ROUND CASSEROLE

Melt 1/4 lb butter in pan and saute until lightly browned: 1/2 C thinly sliced onions, 2 minced cloves garlic, and 1 lb of sliced fresh mushrooms. Add 2 lbs lean ground round and cook till pink disappears.

Stir in 8 T burgundy, 4 T lemon juice, 2 cans consomme, 1 t salt, and 1/4 t pepper. Simmer uncovered 15 mins.

Add 4 C of the thinnest noodles you can find, cover, and cook 10 mins or until tender. Mix in 2 C sour cream, transfer to casserole, and sprinkle generously with chopped parsley. Serve hot with Tossed Green Salad.

BETTY LAND'S MEAT CRUST PIZZA

Mix 1-1/2 lbs ground beef or turkey, 1 lightly beaten egg, 1/2 t ea basil and oregano, and 1/3 C bread or cracker crumbs. Shape into a lightly oiled pie plate.

Layer in the following order: 1 14-oz can tomatoes, chopped and well drained, 1/3 C finely minced onion, 1/2 C small curd cottage cheese, 1 medium zucchini, grated, 1/2 C grated cheddar or Swiss cheese, 1/3 C finely chopped mushrooms, 1/4 C finely chopped green pepper, and 1/4 C sliced pitted olives. Bake in 350 oven for 45 mins. Sprinkle with Parmesan cheese and return to oven for five mins. Serve immediately.

TAIWAN MUSHI

Drain and cube 1 block of tofu into 1/4 in cubes and place in 9x13 in casserole. Saute 1-1/4 lbs lean ground pork, add 1/2 C minced onion, 1/4 C minced bamboo shoots, and add 4 pieces dried mushrooms, sliced. Keep stirring to break up pork.

Combine 1/2 C ea chicken broth and soy and 1-1/2 T sugar and add to meat mixture. Continue cooking about 30 to 45 mins or until liquid has evaporated to about less than half. Cool slightly in sauce, ladle evenly over tofu with perforated spoon. Whisk 3 large eggs, add liquid in which pork was cooked, pour completely over pork mixture, and prick here and there so the eggs will drain into meat and tofu.

Bake in 350 oven about 45 mins or until egg mixture is firm. Do not drain. Let it set, then cut in serving size pieces. Serves 8.

HAMBURGER CUSTARD

Soak 1 slice white bread in a little of 1 C milk, squeeze bread dry back into C of milk, and set aside. Saute 1 chopped onion in 2 T butter, add 1 lb ground beef, and brown lightly. Remove from heat and add 2 T curry, 1 t sugar, 2 t salt, 1/2 t pepper, juice of lemon, and 2 t bitters.

Mix and add bread and 12 finely chopped blanched almonds. Mix thoroughly and turn into buttered casserole. Beat 2 eggs with the reserved milk and pour over meat mixture. Bake in 350 oven until egg and milk have set into a custard… about 25-30 mins. Inserted knife blade should come out clean if done.

Serve with **FANCY STRING BEANS**

Fry strips of bacon until crisp, drain, and crumble.

In some of the fat saute some chopped onions, chopped fresh mushrooms, and slivered almonds. Cook till wilted and drain off fat.

Transfer to saucepan, add just enough moisture to create enough steam when covered. Lay whole tender green beans on top, cover, turn to high, and when it reaches a real boil turn off and leave to steam for 15 mins. Sprinkle bacon on top to serve.

ITALIAN SPAGHETTI

Form 1 lb ground beef into patties, brown in 1/2 C olive oil and break up the meat. Add 2 medium onions finely chopped and saute in oil with 2 medium green peppers finely chopped. Add 1 large can tomatoes, broken up, 1 can tomato paste, 1 can tomato sauce, 1 t ea celery salt, rosemary, and basil, 1/2 t oregano, 1 clove minced garlic, and 1/2 t cayenne. Add 1/2 C red wine and simmer over low heat for 2 hrs, stirring occasionally.

Add 1 small can chopped mushrooms at the last and serve over cooked spaghetti pasta. Hot, buttered, crusty French bread and a Tossed Salad will suffice.

SUPER MEAT LOAF

Combine 1-1/2 lb ground round steak with 3/4 lb pork sausage and add 1/2 C each cottage cheese, dry bread crumbs, and chopped onions, 1/4 C chili sauce, 2 beaten eggs, 1 T ea chopped green pepper and chopped parsley, 1-1/2 t salt, and 1/2 t pepper. Mix well to bind ingredients together.

Line greased 9x5x3 in loaf pan with waxed paper and pack half of the meat mixture into pan. Place 3 peeled, whole hardboiled eggs lengthwise over the center of the meat and cover with the remaining meat mixture. Chill 1 hr, unmold into roasting pan, remove wax paper, and bake in 350 oven for 1 hr or 1 hr and 15 mins.

MEAT LOAF

Chop 1 medium onion and saute in butter. Set aside.

Mix in a bowl: 1/2 C prepared stuffing and 1/2 C bouillon. Add the onion, 1 lb ground beef, 4 sprigs parsley, chopped, 3 T grated Parmesan cheese, 1 beaten egg, 1 t salt, and 1/4 t pepper.

Mix and knead meat and form into a loaf. Dot with butter. Bake 30 mins in 375 oven. Pour 1 8-oz can tomato sauce over loaf and sprinkle 1 t oregano on top. Bake 20 min more.

Serve Meat Loaves with **POTATO PIE.**

In heavy frying pan with lid melt 3-4 T ea oil and oleo. Peel and thinly slice 6 large potatoes, chop 2-3 large onions, and slice 1 lb sharp cheddar cheese.

Cover entire bottom of pan with potatoes, season with S&P, scatter sliced onions on top, and lay sliced cheddar on onions. Repeat layers and top with layer of potatoes, seasoning, and chopped parsley.

Put on lid, cook over lowest heat possible on top of stove till potatoes are fork tender...about 25-35 mins, then remove.

To serve: slice into wedges, lift out with spatula, and turn over onto plate so as to feature the nicely browned bottom.

SMOTHERED MEAT BALLS

Combine 2 lbs ground beef, 1 C bread crumbs, 2 slightly beaten eggs, 1/2 C milk, 2 T chopped parsley, 2 small finely chopped onions, 1 minced clove garlic, and S&P to taste. Mix and shape into small balls, brown in butter, and cover with 2 cans cream of mushroom soup. Bake 1 hr in 350 oven.

Serve with rice and **CARROTS AND PEANUT BUTTER**

Cook sliced carrots until done and puree in blender with peanut butter, S&P and ginger to taste, and a little sour cream to hold together. Reheat to serve.

COMPANY MEAT BALLS

Beat 2 eggs slightly and add: 4 T sauteed chopped onion, 3/4 C milk, 1/4 t pepper, 2 t salt, 1 t ea ginger and curry, and 1-1/2 C bread crumbs. Let stand till crumbs soften, then add 2 lbs. ground round. Knead and shape into small meatballs and brown in oil.

Remove meat balls and stir in 6 T flour, simmer a minute, and gradually add 2 cans beef consomme and 1/2 C rum. Keep stirring till mixture boils and thickens, add meat balls, and simmer 2 mins. Remove to casserole and keep warm in oven.

Serve with either rice or tossed noodles and **HOT HERBED TOMATOES.**

Melt 1-1/4 C butter in pan, stir in 1 t brown sugar, 1/2 t ea salt and either oregano or basil, and dash of pepper. Set 6-8 peeled ripe tomatoes, cut in half if large, stem side down in pan. Cover and simmer 5 mins. Serve with sauce spooned over tomatoes.

BARBECUED MEAT BALLS

Combine 1 lb ground beef, 3/4 C uncooked oatmeal, 1 t salt, 1/8 t pepper, and 2/3 C milk. Mix well and shape into 12 balls. Brown in 2 T fat in skillet, and while meat browns prepare sauce.

BARBECUE SAUCE

Combine 1 C catsup, 2 T ea brown sugar and vinegar, 1 T ea Worcestershire sauce and soy, and 2 t prepared mustard. Pour over meat balls, cover pan, and cook until meat balls are done, about 1/2 hr.

BETTY LAND'S APPLE AND ONION SHORTCAKE

Fry 1/4 lb bacon, cut into bits, and drain on paper. Saute 3 thinly sliced onions in butter for 3 mins and place in casserole. Top with 3 cored, peeled, and sliced tart apples. Cover with 3 T brown sugar and cook over medium heat for 3 mins. Sprinkle with 1/8 t cayenne and salt.

Keep warm while corn bread is baking. Turn heat to low and add 1/2 C ea sour cream and plain yogurt to onions and apples and sprinkle with bacon bits. Keep warm and serve over buttered corn bread.

DR. IMURA'S RICH CORN BREAD

Combine 1-3/4 C Bisquick, 3/4 C sugar, 1/2 C cornmeal, 1/2 T ea baking soda and baking powder, and mix. Combine 1 cube melted butter, 2 slightly beaten eggs, and 1 C buttermilk. Add liquids to dry ingredients, but do not mix too much. Line a 9x9x2 in pan with wax paper and pour in batter. Bake in preheated 350 oven for 25 mins.

ONION PIE

Cook 2 C chopped onions in 1 C butter for 20 mins, but don't let onions brown. Take from stove and cool. Stir in 6 beaten egg yolks, 1/2 C cream, S&P, and 1 C white wine. Stir and fold in beaten whites of the 6 eggs.

Mix each ingredient in slowly and carefully. Fill prepared pie crust with onion mixture and bake for 1/2 hr in 350 oven, or until blade of silver knife comes out clean. The filling should be more than 2 in deep.

Serve hot or cold, but if hot, let it set for at least 10 mins.

HOT SOUPS

At this time of year a nourishing hot soup is welcome, indeed!

HEARTY MEAT SOUP

Wash and drain 1 lb dry kidney beans and put in large pot with 1 smoked ham hock, 2 large beef shanks, 1 lb boneless beef stew meat, 1 crushed clove garlic, 1 large chopped onion, 3 qts water, and 1 8-oz can of tomato sauce. Bring to a boil, reduce heat, and simmer for about 4 hrs or until meat falls off the bones. Discard bones and cool to skim off fat. Add 1 large chopped potato and carrot and cook 30 mins. Add 1 small chopped cabbage and 3/4 C broken raw spaghetti and cook over medium heat till done. Serve with hot garlic bread. Serves 12.

STEPHEN REED'S FRENCH ONION SOUP

In a 3 qt pot saute 5 C thinly sliced Maui onions in 3 T oil until soft, stir in 3 T flour to form paste, add 2 qts bouillon and 1 C bourbon. Season with 1/2 t basil and salt to taste. Simmer 30 to 40 mins, then top with 3 to 6 slices toasted French bread, sprinkle with 1/2 C grated Swiss cheese, and broil until cheese is golden and fluffy. Serve immediately. Serves 6.

FLEMISH TURKEY CHOWDER

Simmer 3 qts water, 3 lbs turkey drumsticks, and 1-1/2 C small dried white beans till turkey and beans are done...about 1-1/4 hrs. Remove turkey meat from bones, return meat to beans and broth. Add 2 t fresh chopped savory, S&P, 1 can each beef broth and light beer, 1 sliced onion, 1/2 lb quartered new potatoes, and cook 30 mins or until vegetables are tender. Serves 12.

FISH CHOWDER STOCK

Simmer a fillet of thawed mahimahi, skin removed, in sufficient water to cover until done. Skim and put aside. Fry chopped pork or bacon, add chopped onions and cubed potatoes, and simmer with water from fish until potatoes are done. Add broken up pieces of fish, season with dill, marjoram, and S&P to taste, and freeze. Or add cream, half-and-half, and milk and heat to boiling point to serve with Saloon Pilot crackers. Keep fish chowder stock in the freezer until ready to use, then just thaw, add half-and-half and milk, check seasoning, and heat.

RICH POTATO SOUP

Bake 5 large potatoes.

In a large pot combine 2 C peeled and diced baked potatoes with 2 medium onions, diced, 1/4 C butter, and 8 C water. Bring to a boil, lower heat and simmer, stirring occasionally, till potatoes soften and make a thick broth.

Remove from heat and add another 4 C diced cooked potatoes, 1 C diced green onions, 1 t garlic powder, 2 chicken bouillon cubes, 1/2 t salt, and 1/2 C chopped chives.

In a blender container combine 1 C sour cream, 1 3-oz package softened cream cheese, 1 C milk, and 1/4 lb shredded mild cheddar cheese, and blend till smooth. Add this to soup, return to heat, and simmer over very low heat until hot but not boiling. Stir constantly, taste for seasoning, and serve hot. Garnish with parsley. Yields 4-1/2 qts nourishing soup.

If you like curry, add a tablespoon or two into the blended mixture.

CURRIED CHICKEN SOUP

Melt 1/4 C butter in pot, add 1 minced onion and 1 peeled and chopped tart apple, and cook until limp. Stir in 3 T flour, 1-1/2 T curry, 1/4 t ginger, S&P to taste, and add 3 C chicken broth. Stir and add 2 C bite-size pieces of cooked chicken. Bake in 350 oven for 30 mins. Add half-and-half if too thick.

Serve soup with bowls of coarsely chopped salted peanuts, chopped hardboiled egg, chopped chives, and chutney. Serves 4.

CHINESE PORK MEAT BALL SOUP

Combine and form into walnut size balls: 1/2 lb ground lean pork, 1/2 t salt, 1 green onion finely chopped, 1 T cornstarch, 1 egg, dash of pepper, and 1 t grated ginger root.

Soup Base: boil up 4 C stock and add meat balls. Cook 5-7 mins, then add 3 chopped mushrooms, 1 green onion, chopped, dash S&P, 1 T soy, and 1 lightly beaten egg while stirring. Cover and cook 1 min.

HAM POTATO CHOWDER

Cook 1 C ea chopped onion and celery with 1 minced clove garlic in 2 T butter until tender but not brown. Add 2 C cut-up ham, 2 C diced potatoes, 1 bay leaf, 1/2 t ea thyme and tabasco, 2 C water, and cook until potatoes are done. Add 2 C milk, 1 can stewed tomatoes, drained and cut up, and heat to boiling to serve. Serves 4-6.

LENTIL SOUP

Heat 1-1/2 T oil in large pot, saute 2 to 3 chopped onions and 3 grated carrots with 3/4 t each marjoram and thyme. Cook and stir until limp. Add 1 28-oz can tomatoes with juice, coarsely chopped, 7 C beef broth, and 1-1/2 C dried lentils rinsed and picked over. Bring to a boil, reduce heat, cover pot, and simmer 1 hr or until lentils are tender. Add S&P to taste, 6 oz white wine, 1/3 C chopped parsley, and simmer a few mins. Serve in bowls piping hot with grated cheddar sprinkled on each serving, and pass the French bread.

BLACK BEAN SOUP

Combine 1 C soaked and drained black beans, 1 ham bone, 2 chopped up celery stalks, 2 chopped onions, 1 qt water, cover, and cook 3-1/2 hrs or until beans are soft. Remove bone, chop up meat, return to pot, and add 1 t salt, 1/8 t each pepper and dry mustard, 2 T margarine, 3/4 T flour, and stir well. Add 3 T or more sherry, cook to heat through, and serve with slice of lemon. Serves 6.

KAMAAINA PORTUGUESE BEAN SOUP

Cover 2 to 3 ham hocks with water, bring to boil, cook 10 mins., drain, and discard water. Refill pot with water to cover hocks and boil until tender. Remove meat from fat and bones and return to pot. Add 3 large cans red kidney beans, 1 diced potato, 1 diced carrot, 2 chopped onions, 1 large can stewed tomatoes, 2 minced cloves garlic, and 2 Portuguese sausages, sliced.

Season to taste with paprika or cayenne, and simmer for 30 to 45 mins. or until vegetables are done. If soup is too thick, add consomme or V-8 Juice to your liking.

Ten mins before serving add small head of shredded cabbage, and if you like 1 C cooked macaroni. Simmer to serve hot in large bowls with crusty, warm French bread.

FRUITS

AVOCADO OR ALLIGATOR PEAR

Available year-round, easily digestible, but high in calories! They are ripe when soft to the touch or tooth pick inserted in stem end goes in easily.

Brush cut avocado with lemon to keep from turning brown.

Leave pit in unused half of avocado and store in refrigerator.

Place seed on top of pureed avocado until serving time and cover securely with Saran Wrap.

For Rings: cut in half crosswise, remove pit and slice crosswise.

For Balls: scoop out unpeeled halves with melon baller.

Avocados are a great addition to tossed salads.

Combine with pomelo, orange, or grapefruit sections and toss with dressing of 1/2 C catsup, juice of 2 limes, tabasco, and sugar to taste.

Fill avocado halves with your favorite chicken salad, place on lettuce leaves, and sprinkle top with chopped macadamia nuts.

Sandwich Spread: peel an avocado, remove seed and inner skin, puree, add 1 T lemon juice, 1 t garlic salt, 1 T A-1 Sauce, dash paprika, and stir to blend. Chill.

Guacamole: puree 2 avocados with 1 t season salt, 1 T lemon juice, and Worcestershire sauce to taste. Place seed on top to keep from turning brown.

For dinner starter serve avocado balls marinated in white wine with seedless grapes.

Sprinkle cubed avocado with lime juice and crumblings of Roquefort cheese, and add last minute to tossed green salad.

Add cubes or balls of avocado to consomme.

Plain ketchup is a popular sauce when eating a half an avocado, but some prefer sprinkling sugar over theirs.

BLENDER AVOCADO CHEESECAKE

Prepare a graham cracker crust.

In electric blender puree the flesh of an avocado, 8-oz package softened cream cheese, 1/2 C sour cream, and 3 or 4 strips lemon peel. Process till smooth, add 1-3/4 oz vanilla flavored instant pudding, and blend just until mixed. Pour into crust and chill several hrs till set. Serves 6.

STUFFED AVOCADO

Halve avocados, fill with vinegar and pieces of garlic, and let stand 1/2 hr. Empty and fill with rich cream sauce mixed with crab, lobster, shrimp, or chicken, season well, and cover with Parmesan cheese. Bake in 350 oven until heated through.

AVOCADO SPREAD

Peel 1 ripe avocado, mash pulp, and combine with 1 3-oz package softened cream cheese, 1-1/2 t lemon juice, 1 t onion salt, and 2 t sherry. Blend well, cover, and chill. Serve with assorted crackers or large Fritos.

BANANA

Banana is referred to as the "tree of birth and life" or "life out of death." As the fruit destroys the tree, new plants spring up from the old stumps.

The banana knows no season, is one of the most important and popular fruits grown in the Islands, and can be used in soups, salads, entrees, baked goods, and desserts.

It is a food rich in carbohydrates and other nutritives, particularly potassium.

If a hand of bananas ripens all at one time, you may put them in the refrigerator and it doesn't damage the fruit or change its flavor.

An overabundance of ripe bananas may be frozen as is in Ziploc bags, or mashed with a little lemon juice and frozen to use later in cakes, breads, slushes, or when whole baked or fried. Or fry up a batch of bananas in butter, freeze, and re-heat later.

Combined with peanut butter, mashed bananas make a delicious filling for sandwiches.

Slice bananas into your next batch of pancake batter or over bowls of cereal.

FRIED BANANAS

Remove skin and strings from banana, cut in half crosswise and lengthwise, sprinkle with S&P and lemon juice, dip in crumbs, and fry in deep fat slowly, turning to brown and cook evenly.

BAKED BANANAS

BAKING BANANAS can not be eaten raw. The most popular varieties are the Popoulu and Maiamaoli.

Bake cooking bananas whole. Cut off both ends, place in pan with a little water, and bake in 350 oven till skins pop open and they are soft. To serve: remove skin, place pulp in casserole, douse with lots of butter, and serve warm as a starch.

Or Bake Bananas, serve in skins to keep warm, and pass the butter.

BAKED BANANAS IN RUM

Simmer 1 C sugar, 1/2 C lemon juice, and 1 T butter 10 mins, then add 1 T white rum. Peel 6 medium size under-ripe bananas, slice in half, and place in buttered baking dish, cut side down. Pour syrup over, bake 30 mins in 400 oven, and turn once after 15 mins. Serve hot in dessert dishes with ice cream or whipped cream.

15

TWO GRAIN BANANA BREAD

Heat oven to 350 and grease bottom only of 9x5 in loaf pan.

Beat together: 1 C mashed ripe bananas, 3/4 C milk, 3/4 C firmly packed brown sugar, 2 eggs, 1/2 C vegetable oil, and add 1-1/3 C each whole wheat and white flour sifted with 4 t baking powder and 1 t salt, and 1 C quick or old-fashioned oats, 1/2 C chopped walnuts, and mix just until dry ingredients are moistened. Pour into prepared pan and bake about 1 hr or until pick comes out clean. Cool 10 mins, then cool completely on wire rack.

BANANA DATE BRAN BREAD

Sift together 2-1/2 C flour, 1 t salt, and 2-1/2 t baking powder.

Beat 1/2 C shortening and 3/4 C sugar till creamy, add 2 eggs, and beat until light and fluffy. Stir in 1 C chopped pecans, 1/2 C mashed banana, 1 C pitted and snipped dates, and 1 C bran cereal.

Alternately add 1/2 C milk and the flour mixture. Turn batter into greased pan, bake in 350 oven about 1 hr, cool in pan 10 mins, then remove to rack to cook.

EDEE SEYMOUR'S NUTTY BANANA MUFFINS

Preheat oven to 425 and grease muffin cups.

Combine 2 C pancake mix, 1/4 C sugar, 1/4 t cinnamon, 1/2 C chopped nuts (pecans, macadamia, walnut or whatever), and stir in 3/4 C milk, 1/2 C mashed ripe bananas, and 3 T oil or 1/2 stick melted butter. Stir only until combined. Fill cups 3/4 full and bake 15 to 20 mins. Serves 12.

BANANA LEMON LOAF

Preheat oven to 350 and grease 2 loaf pans or one bundt pan.

Cream 1/2 C shortening and 1 C sugar, blend in 2 beaten eggs, 1-1/2 C mashed ripe bananas, and 6 T lemon juice, and stir in 2 C flour mixed with 1 t baking soda and 1 T salt. Add 2 to 3 T grated lemon peel. Pour into pans and bake 1 hr.

COCONUT

The coconut is Hawaii's multi-use fruit! Besides being a staple food, it can be used for buttons, houses, utensils, calabashes, and boats. The coconut liquid is called water. Milk is the net result of pouring (1/2 C) boiling water or milk over (3 C) grated coconut meat in double thicknesses of cheese cloth, soaking this for 20 mins, and squeezing the liquid all out until meat is dry.

The meat of a young green coconut is soft and sweet, and a treat to simply spoon out and enjoy. When fully ripe, the coconut meat is hard and crunchy.

Curry isn't curry unless you use coconut cream in the sauce and freshly grated coconut for a condiment.

Once grated, fresh coconut can be used in a variety of recipes.

Add it to your favorite waffle recipe and serve with coconut syrup.

Sprinkle freshly grated coconut over an Island fruit cocktail.

Make a prepared boxed vanilla cream pie according to directions and add grated coconut and sliced bananas. Pour into prepared pie shell and top with whipped cream and more grated coconut.

Grated coconut is the piece de resistance of a fresh coconut cake. Make your favorite box or "from scratch" recipe, bake in two round layers, and cool. Top bottom layer with a thick custard sauce, cover with second layer, and cover cake completely with 7-minute frosting. Sprinkle top and sides generously with grated coconut. Keep refrigerated.

COCONUT SHORTBREAD COOKIES

Cream 1 C butter and 3 T sugar, add 2 C sifted flour, 1 C grated coconut, and 1 t of vanilla, and mix well. Form into 2 rolls as for icebox cookies, wrap in wax paper, and thoroughly chill. Slice 1/4 in thick and bake 30 to 35 mins at 300 on ungreased cookie sheet. Remove while warm and sprinkle with sifted powdered sugar.

COCONUT PUDDING

Heat 1-1/2 C coconut milk or plain milk, add 3 T sugar and 2 T cornstarch, and stir well. When it begins to boil and thicken, add 2 stiffly beaten egg whites, cool, and add 1/2 C grated coconut. Mix well and pour into mold. Chill to serve.

CURRY SERVED IN COCONUT SHELLS

Use only green coconuts with spoon custard meat inside. Whack off top of husk and enough of the nut to fill it with a serving of chicken or shrimp curry. Replace the top and seal with a paste of flour and water. Set in pan of water and put in 350 oven for about 1 hr, basting with water to keep the coconut from burning.

Place coconuts before each guest and let them help themselves to the rice and vegetables, and pass the condiments after everyone has ladled out their own curry.

HAUPIA

Pour 4-1/2 C boiling water over 4 C grated coconut and let stand for about 20 mins. Strain through several thicknesses of cheesecloth. Cook coconut milk over medium heat up to boiling point, but do not allow to boil. Combine 1-1/2 C sugar and 1 C cornstarch with 1/2 C fresh milk, and stir until smooth. Add this mixture to the coconut mixture slowly, stirring constantly until it thickens. Let it cook a few minutes longer. Pour into square pans, cool until it sets, then cut in serving squares. Refrigerate.

SURINAM CHERRY

Suddenly you will find this feathery leafed tree loaded with small ribbed fruit ranging in color from yellow, orange, red and plum-colored. The soft and juicy flesh surrounds a single large seed, and is mostly acid to taste.

SURINAM CHERRY JAM

Wash and clean 2 C ripe cherries, put in pot with just enough water to barely see through. Mash down and stew gently for about 1/2 hr. Put through ricer and combine cup of pulp for cup of sugar, bring to boil, and simmer 15 mins or until mixture sheets from spoon. Pour in sterilized jars.

This can be used for cold meats, too, besides on toast.

Use the puree as a concentrated fruit juice base. It adds a delicious flavor when combined with other Island fruit juices.

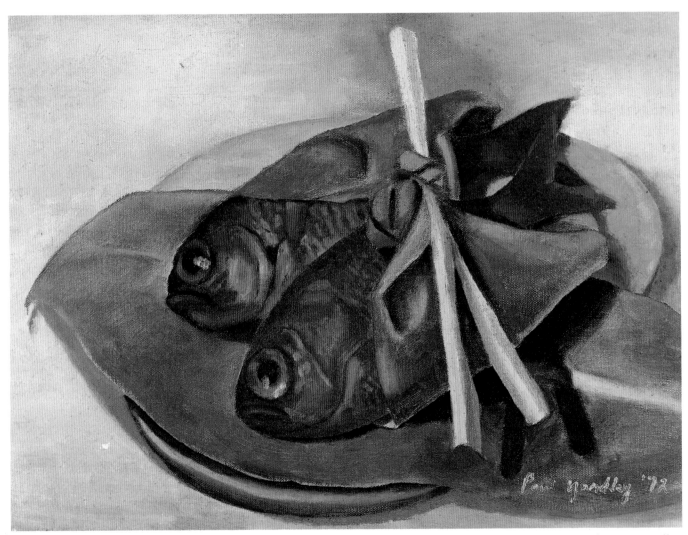

Red Fish in Ti Leaf   *Courtesy of Louise Yardley*

FEBRUARY

◆

*It's February and time for
hearts and flowers.*

Remember the 14th is Valentine's Day with "Sweets for the Sweet".

Ash Wednesday generally falls in February and heralds the six week period of Lent. For some, fish becomes an important part of the menu on Fridays.

Be on the alert for the sagging Soursop trees!

DESSERT TREATS

Top rich vanilla ice cream with generous helping of either Amaretto liqueur or Scotch whiskey.

Top strawberry ice cream with Tripple Sec, and French vanilla is enhanced with Creme de Cacao.

Jazz up coffee ice cream by melting it just enough to fold in 1 C dark rum and 1 C broken chocolate chips. Return to freezer or spoon into parfait glasses and freeze until ready to serve.

Pour green Creme de Menthe over lemon sherbet in parfait glasses. Top with cherry and keep frozen.

Crush broken pieces of peanut brittle with rolling pin until they are smallish chunks, then blend them into slightly melted rich vanilla ice cream and re-freeze. Or use Almond Roca broken into chips.

ICE CREAM PIE

Crust: Combine 1 C corn flake crumbs with 1/3 C melted margarine and 3 T sugar. Press into 8 or 9 in pie dish and refrigerate for hour or so.

Filling: Combine 1 qt vanilla ice cream with 1 small can of thawed lemonade. Pour into crust and leave in freezer. Remove 15 min before serving time.

STEPHEN REED'S CHOCOLATE MOUSSE

Melt 8 oz semisweet chocolate, 5 T strong coffee, 1 T dark Jamaica rum, and 4 T cognac over double boiler, stirring until blended. Add 1/4 C sugar and stir until smooth and glistening.

Remove from heat and cool. Whip 2 C whipping cream till very stiff, stir in 1 T sugar and 1 t vanilla, and fold in chocolate mixture. Chill. Serves 6.

LEMON PUDDING

Combine 1 C sugar, 1/8 t salt, 1/4 C flour, and 2 T melted oleo. Add 4 to 5 T lemon juice and 1 T grated lemon peel. Stir in 2 well beaten egg yolks and 1 C scalded milk. Mix well. Fold in 2 stiffly beaten egg whites and pour into greased 1-1/2 qt casserole. Bake in pan with 1 in hot water for 1 hr in 325 oven.

Sponge cake comes to top and layer of lemon custard forms on bottom. If it curdles it will be all right after baking.

CREME BRULEE
(BURNT CREME CUSTARD)

Heat 1 pt whipping cream over low heat until bubbles form around edge of pan. Beat 4 egg yolks with 1/2 C granulated sugar together for 3 mins. Beat cream gradually into egg yolks. Bake in custard cups in pan with 1/2 in water for 45 mins to an hr in 325 oven.

Sprinkle 2 t sugar over each custard and broil until medium brown. Chill to serve. Serves 6.

MICHELE FERGUSON'S BOULES DE NEIGE
(SNOW BALLS)

Bring 1 qt of milk, 1/4 t vanilla, and 5 T sugar to a boil. Separate 5 eggs, add pinch of cream of tartar to the whites, and whisk until stiff. Drop by tablespoons into boiling milk over medium heat. Shape into a ball, cook 1 min, turn, cook 1 more min or until puffed up. Remove from the milk with slotted spoon and let drain of all liquid. Cook all the egg whites this way.

Add 5 egg yolks to 8 oz sugar and whisk until mixture is pale yellow. Pour into it 1/4 C of the hot milk a little at a time and whisk vigorously. Return cream sauce to pan, cook until it thickens, but do not boil. Cool. Serve custard topped with snow balls. Sprinkle with toasted almonds. Refrigerate until serving. Serves 6.

JUNE HUMME'S CHOCOLATE
BREAD PUDDING

Combine 1 C milk with 1 T melted butter, 3 slices bread, cubed, 5 T chocolate, 1-1/2 C sugar, and 3 egg yolks.

Boil 1 C milk and pour mixture into it to cook until thick. Pour into buttered baking dish. Beat 3 egg whites until stiff, add 1/2 t vanilla and 1-1/2 T sugar, and spoon meringue on top of pudding. Bake in 350 oven until meringue browns.

RICE PUDDING

Scald 1 pt milk and add 1-1/2 C boiled rice. Beat 3 egg yolks, add 1/2 C sugar, and gradually add the scalded milk and rice. Place in double boiler and cook until mixture thickens, stirring constantly. Remove, add 1 t vanilla, and pour into baking dish.

Beat whites of 3 eggs until stiff, add 3 T sugar, and beat thoroughly. Pour over rice mixture, place in oven and brown. Serve hot or cold with cream.

BREAD PUDDING

Scald 1 qt milk. Beat yolks of 4 eggs with 1 C sugar, 1/2 t salt, and 1 t vanilla. Add 2 C bread crumbs, moistened and squeezed dry. Slowly add the scalded milk and pour into baking dish. Bake for 15 mins. Sprinkle with 1/2 C raisins and return to oven to bake 15 mins longer. Remove, sprinkle with bits of jelly or jam. Beat 4 egg whites until stiff, add 2 T sugar, and beat well. Spread on top of pudding and bake until brown. Serve hot or cold with cream.

FRUITY TREATS

Soak seedless red or green grapes in a bowl of water and ice for an hour, then drain and leave in refrigerator for crunchiness.

GRAPES IN SOUR CREAM

Prepare this the morning of serving. Pick over clusters of seedless grapes and pick each one off individually, discard any soft or bad ones. Cover them in enough whipped sour cream to really coat each grape, then sprinkle with dark brown sugar to taste. Refrigerate and keep stirring whenever you're at the refrigerator. Sprinkle 1/4 C brown sugar over the top of grapes just before serving and place under the broiler very briefly, just enough to caramelize the sugar. Green seedless grapes are better.

Sections of grapefruit become a snappy dessert when combined with green Creme de Menthe and fresh mint leaves topped with a green cherry.

BAKED GRAPEFRUIT WITH SHERRY

Halve and section grapefruit, fill center with maple syrup, and let stand. Put under the broiler for a few minutes to serve. When browned, serve with a dollop of sherry in each.

APPLE SAUCE

Chop up crisp, green apples into saucepan, add just enough water to keep from burning the bottom, and add sugar and cinnamon to taste. Simmer gently until mushy, put through ricer, and refrigerate. This is good over banana bread with a bit of vanilla ice cream, yogurt, or whipped cream.

APPLE SAUCE

Combine 1 can applesauce (or homemade) with 1/2 pt whipped cream and 1/2 C dark rum. Stir just lightly enough to blend and spoon into dessert bowls. To serve, sprinkle brown sugar over the top and add dollops of whipped cream.

HAUPIA GUAVA TARTS

Prepare 6 tart shells.

Combine 1/4 C thawed coconut milk with 5 T cornstarch and 1/4 C sugar to form a paste. Bring 2-3/4 C thawed coconut milk to boil and gradually add cornstarch mixture, stirring constantly. Cook until mixture thickens, cool slightly, and pour into tart shells. Chill in refrigerator.

Guava Topping: Blend 2 T sugar and 1 T cornstarch, slowly stir in 2/3 C guava nectar, and cook over low flame until thick, stirring constantly. Pour over chilled haupia, chill, and serve.

RUM CREAM PIE

Prepare pie shell.

Beat 6 egg yolks until they are light and add 1 C sugar.

Soak 1 T gelatine in 1/2 C cold water, put over low flame and let it come to a boil, then pour over egg and sugar mixture, stirring briskly.

Whip 1 pt cream until stiff, fold it into the egg mixture, and flavor with 1/2 C Jamaica rum. Cool and pour into shell. When the filling has set, sprinkle the top with shaved Baker's unsweetened chocolate squares.

This will make 2 smaller pies and is more than enough to fill a 9-inch shell.

NANCY VERACRUZ'S YOGURT PIE

Prepare 1 large graham cracker crust.

Combine 2 cartons boysenberry, blueberry, or strawberry yogurt thoroughly mixed with a large container of Cool Whip. Pour into crust, and freeze 1 hr before serving. If frozen longer, defrost before serving.

YUMMY PUMPKIN ICE CREAM PIE

Prepare 1 9-in pastry shell, baked, or 1 graham cracker crust shell.

Combine 1/4 C honey or brown sugar, 3/4 C pumpkin puree, 1/2 t cinnamon, and 1/4 t ea ginger and salt and bring just to the boil, stirring constantly. Cool, then beat in 1 qt vanilla ice cream, softened, and 1/2 C macadamia nuts, chopped, and pour into crust. Freeze until ready to serve, then garnish with 1 C heavy whipping cream, whipped, and top with sprinkle of nutmeg.

NORMA JOINER'S CHOCOLATE DELIGHT

Crust: cream 1 block each butter and margarine with 3 T powdered sugar, add 3/4 C chopped nuts and 1-1/2 C flour. Press into 9x13 in pan and bake at 425 for 8 to 10 mins. Cool.

Filling: beat 1-1/2 C powdered sugar and 2 packages (8-oz each) cream cheese until smooth. Add 3/4 of 1 carton (13-1/2 oz) Cool Whip and mix well until blended together. Do not beat.

Spread on cooled crust and refrigerate at least 3 hrs.

Pudding: Combine 2 packages chocolate instant pudding mix and 3 C cold milk and whip till thick. Pour over set cream cheese mixture and spread remaining 1/4 tub of Cool Whip on top. Sprinkle with nuts or chopped cherries and refrigerate.

KAMUELA'S PEANUT BUTTER PIE

Cream together 1 8-oz package softened cream cheese, 1/2 C chunky peanut butter, and 1/2 C confectioner's sugar. Fold in 12-oz carton of Cool Whip. Pour into prepared pie shell and refrigerate.

Pie Crust: mix 1-1/2 C flour with 1/2 C oil, 2 T milk, 1-1/2 T sugar and 1/2 t salt. Mix with hands, press down with fingers in pie shell. Bake 10 mins in 450 oven.

This dessert also freezes well.

AVOCADO PIE

Prepare graham cracker pie shell.

Line pie shell with 1/4 C sour cream...or more.

Filling: mash 1 medium size avocado, add 1 can Bordens condensed milk and 1/3 C fresh lemon juice and blend in blender. Place in pie shell, chill until firm. (At this point pie may be frozen.) 15 mins before serving, top with Cool Whip or whipped cream.

QUICK COCONUT CAKE

Combine 1 box yellow cake mix, 1 t baking powder, 2 eggs, 1-1/2 C coconut milk and beat with electric beater for 2 mins at high speed. Fold in 1 C shredded coconut. Bake in 9x11x2 in pan in 325 oven for 35-45 mins.

Frosting: Beat 1 bottle whipping Avoset with 1/4 C sugar and 1/2 t vanilla. Frost cake and sprinkle grated coconut on top and sides. Chill.

EASY COCONUT CAKE FROSTING

Mix up a carton of sour cream with a box of confectioner's powdered sugar, add 2 C thawed frozen coconut, mix, and frost plain cake.

CHOCOLATE CHIP CAKE

Combine and mix in a bowl: 1 package chocolate fudge cake mix, 1 small package chocolate pudding mix, 1 C sour cream, 4 eggs, 1/2 C warm water, 1/2 C oil, and 3 T melted butter. Add 1 large package chocolate chips by hand, mix, and put in well greased bundt pan. Bake 50-60 mins at 350. Test with finger (not toothpick) in center of cake.

After baking, leave in pan 10-15 min, then turn on rack. Serve warm or cold.

HARUKO FUJI'S PUDDING CAKE

Freeze 1 large Hershey Chocolate Bar.

Crust: Combine 1 C chopped walnuts, almonds or macadamia nuts with 1 C flour and 1 block melted butter. Mix and pat into 13x9x2 in pan. Bake in 350 oven 10-20 mins and cool.

Filling: Cream 1 8-oz package cream cheese with 1 C powdered sugar and fold in 1 C Cool Whip. Mix and spread evenly over crust.

Combine 1 package of chocolate instant pudding and 1 package vanilla instant pudding with 3 C milk. Mix according to directions and spread over cream cheese.

Spread remaining Cool Whip on top, grate 1 large Hershey Chocolate Bar on top and chill.

GRACE MORIMOTO'S JELLO CREAM CAKE

Crust: cut 3/4 C butter into 1-1/2 C flour with pastry blender. Add 1/2 C chopped nuts and mix together. Press evenly into a 9x13 in pan. Bake at 350 for 15-20 mins till lightly browned. Cool.

Filling: Dissolve 1 box lime Jello in 1 C hot water and cool. Cream 1 8-oz cream cheese and 3/4 C sugar. Blend in cooled Jello and fold in 1 C Cool Whip. Pour into cooled crust and chill until firm...about 1 to 2 hrs.

Topping: Dissolve 2 boxes strawberry Jello in 3 C hot water and cool. Pour carefully over cream cheese mixture and refrigerate to set. Top with Cool Whip.

CARROT CAKE A LA GIGI

Cream together 1-1/2 C oil, 1-1/2 C sugar (or 1 C honey), and 2 eggs.

Combine 2-1/2 C flour, 1 t soda, 1/2 t salt, 1 t ea cinnamon and vanilla, and add to cream mixture.

Add 2 C grated carrots, 1 C crushed pineapple, 1 C chopped nuts, and mix well. Pour into bundt pan or 9x13 in pan (grease and flour bottom of pan). Bake 40-45 mins in 350 oven.

Frosting: Cream 1 3-oz package cream cheese and 1/2 C oleo or butter with 3/4 box of powdered sugar and add 1 t vanilla. Blend well and frost the cake.

GRACE MORIMOTO'S HAWAIIAN DELIGHT

Follow directions on 1 package yellow cake mix, but substitute pineapple juice for amount of water called for. Bake according to directions in 13x10x2 in pan. Soften and stir down 1 8-oz package cream cheese, gradually add 1 box instant vanilla pudding until it is smooth consistency. Add 1 C cold milk, stir till smooth and thick. Add 1 2-oz can crushed pineapple (strained) and 1 C whipped cream topping. Blend, mix and spread on cooled cake. Garnish with whipped cream topping and sprinkle with chopped nuts.

THE WILLOW'S GUAVA CAKE

Sift 6 C flour, 4 T baking powder, and 1 t salt together.

Beat 1 lb butter and 3 C sugar until creamy. Add 6 eggs gradually until mixed well with butter mixture. Add the flour mixture alternately with 2 C guava juice. Mix well, but do not over-mix.

Turn batter into two 9x12 in greased pans and bake at 350 for 15 mins or until done.

DUMP CAKE

Preheat oven to 350. Grease 9x13 in pan.

Spread 1 21-oz can cherry pie filling evenly on the bottom of pan. Layer 1 20-oz can crushed pineapple, undrained, on top, sprinkle 1 18-1/2-oz package yellow cake mix over, and cover with 2 sticks of melted butter. Top with 1 C ea flaked coconut and chopped nuts.

Bake about 1 hr or until done. Serve with ice cream or whipped cream.

KALISA CHOW'S APPLE CRUNCH CAKE

Clean, pare, core, and chop 6 apples into pot. Cover slightly with a little water and flavor with cinnamon to taste. Cook until apples are soft. Turn into 9x13 in glass pan. Cool, sprinkle 1 box yellow cake mix over apples to cover completely, then dot generously with pats of butter over the top. Bake in 350 oven until golden brown...about 25-30 mins.

POPULAR FISH IN HAWAII

AHI Yellow Fin Tuna: sold in chunks usually; raw, especially for sashimi; fry, bake or broil.

AKU Bonito (Tuna): raw for sashimi or poki; dry or fry.

AKULE Big-Eyed Scad: usually found in large schools close to shore; excellent dried, raw, fried or broiled.

AMA'AMA Mullet: formerly raised and fattened in fish ponds; sweet, fat, white meat especially delicious eaten raw; bake or broil in ti leaves; steam; for clear soup.

A'U Marlin, Swordfish: lean meat; marinate and broil or fry.

AWEOWEO Red fish with big eyes: superstition is that when schools of this fish enter a harbor, it means great sorrow ahead - as in the day a large school entered Honolulu harbor and President Franklin D. Roosevelt and Princess Abigail Kawananakoa died. Either fry or broil; dry.

KAWAKAWA Bonito: best raw for poki; fry or broil.

KUMU Goatfish: great delicacy; tabu to women in olden days; delicious raw; broil or steam in ti leaves.

MAHIMAHI Dolphin: sportsmen's fish; most popular with malihinis and kamaainas alike for its sweet, mild meat; saute or broil.

MOI Thread Fin: found in shallow waters along the shore and caught by throw net; sweet, delicious; steam or bake whole. In the olden days, only the royalty were allowed to eat this fish.

NENUE Delicacy; best raw or broiled in ti leaves; fry.

OI'O Bonefish (bony as the name implies): best made into fish cakes by scraping flesh off the bones; old-timers lomi raw meat with limu, kukui nut, and a little water.

ONO Wahoo (Mackerel type): quick fry or broil; good for chowder and sashimi.

OPAKAPAKA Pink Snapper: delicious, sweet white meat; raw, dry, fry, bake whole in ti leaves, or steam.

OPELU Mackerel: raw, dry, fry, or broil.

UHU Parrot Fish: favorite of old-timers for its sweet meat in raw fish; dry or broil.

ULUA Jack Crevalle: several varieties; fishermen's delight; raw, bake or broil.

WEKE Fish like Kumu: pan fry in butter; bake whole if large; broil quickly. The young fish are called O'Ama. Schools of O'Ama near shore attract many fishermen with bamboo poles and are easily and quickly caught.

FISH

Fish is a great source of low-fat protein, is low in calories, and some research indicates that including fish regularly in your diet helps protect you against heart disease.

Fish is highly perishable, so keep it well chilled at all times. It's best cooked the day of purchase, but can be kept 24 hours at the most. When buying fish, remember that fresh fish does not smell, and if considering a whole fish be sure the eyes are clear and bulging, the gills bright red, and the scales tight against the body. The flesh should be firm to the touch.

You can eat fish raw, baked, broiled in the oven or over charcoal, fried, steamed or poached, and then there's always chowder.

It's better under-cooked than over-cooked. Learn to choose fresh fish with care, preserve it well, and cook with respect to really enjoy.

BAKED FISH

Rinse a 2 lb whole, cleaned, fresh fish and rub inside and out with Hawaiian salt. Rinse off and pat dry. Slather the whole fish with a mixture of 1/2 C mayonnaise, 1 T ea soy and lemon juice, 1/2 t dill, and wrap securely in aluminum foil. Bake 40 mins in 350 oven, test for doneness, and cook longer if needed.

BAKED FISH IN TI LEAVES

Lay whole, cleaned fish on bed of several wet ti leaves, place slices of lemon and onion in belly and on top, and sprinkle with Hawaiian salt to taste. Wrap securely with more ti leaves, tie each end and middle securely, and place in pan with a bit of water. Allow 15 to 20 mins per lb in 350 oven.

BAKED STUFFED OPAKAPAKA

Make your favorite stuffing and let it cool.

Rinse and pat dry 1 whole 4-6 lb fish. Stuff belly with the dressing and secure with skewers. Rub with oil or mayonnaise, place in pan, cover lightly with foil, and bake about 40 min in 350 oven. Remove foil, test for doneness, and return to oven for 10 more mins to make it brown and crispy.

BAKED FISH FILLETS PARMESAN

Saute 2 T finely chopped onions in 1/4 C butter for 5 mins. Blend in 1/4 C flour, add 1 C chicken stock, and 1/4 C white wine. Continue cooking and stirring until mixture boils and thickens. Stir in 1/4 C Parmesan cheese, 1 T chopped parsley, 1 t lemon juice, and S&P.

Thaw 1 lb frozen fish fillets (perch or sole), arrange in greased shallow baking dish, pour sauce over, and dust with paprika. Bake in 450 oven for 10 to 15 mins or till fish flakes when tested with fork. Serves 4.

SAUTEED MAHIMAHI

Combine 1/2 C each flour and dry bread crumbs, 1/2 t salt, and dash of pepper. Cut 2 lbs mahimahi into 1-1/2 inch chunks, dip in 2 beaten eggs, and dredge in flour mixture.

Heat 1/2 C butter in large frying pan, saute fish over medium high heat, turning to brown all sides...about 10 mins. Remove fish to a heated serving platter and keep warm.

De-glaze pan with 1/4 C dry white wine and keep stirring to cook another 3 mins. Add 4 T more butter and saute 1 C coarsely chopped macadamia nuts until golden brown. Pour this over fish and garnish with sprigs of parsley and lemon wedges. Serve immediately.

ELENA ATKINS' MACADAMIA NUT MAHIMAHI

Season 12 2-oz slices mahimahi fillets with S&P and place in greased casserole. Melt 1/4 C butter in saucepan, stir in 4 T flour, and cook 1 min. Add 1 C ea coconut milk and half-and-half and stir. Add 1/4 C white wine, stirring constantly. Simmer several minutes. Pour sauce over fish and sprinkle chopped macadamias over the fish. Add some wine around the edges and bake at 375 for 20 mins. Garnish with parsley and lemon.

BEER BATTER FISH

Beat 2 egg yolks with 1 C cold beer, sift in 1 C flour, and blend well. Set aside.

Dip 2 lbs fish fillets in beer, then flour, shake off excess, then dip into batter and place in hot vegetable oil to fry until golden brown. Remove and drain on paper towels.

SYLVIA PABLO'S SOUR CREAM FISH BAKE

Wash, pat dry, and cut 3 lbs mahimahi or ulua into serving pieces. Place in shallow baking dish, pour 1 C sherry over top and marinate for 15 mins on each side. Discard juice, pour 1/4 C melted butter over fish, and sprinkle 1/4 t ea salt and Aji, 1/4 t pepper, dash of paprika, and broil 10 mins. Baste with pan juices and set aside to cool slightly.

Mix 1/2 can cream of shrimp soup and 1/2 C ea sour cream and chopped round onion, and pour on top of fish. Sprinkle with chopped macadamia nuts and paprika. When ready to serve, bake in 250 oven for 30 mins to heat through.

FISH CAKES

Combine 3 C scraped raw white fish, 1 C cornstarch, and 3 unbeaten eggs. In another bowl mix together 1-1/2 to 2 C water, 5 t salt, 6 T sugar, 3 t Aji, 1 carrot cut into very thin strips, and 1/2 C finely chopped water chestnuts. Add this slowly to fish mixture, spoon out by tablespoons and drop into hot deep fat or oil, and cook on both sides until cakes turn to light golden brown. Drain cakes on paper towels and serve hot. 20 cakes.

FISH SOUFFLE

Make a cream sauce with 3 T ea butter and flour, add 2 C light cream or half-and-half, and season to taste. Remove from stove and stir in 4 well beaten egg yolks and 2 C flaked fish. Cool to lukewarm. Fold in 4 stiffly beaten egg whites, pour into greased casserole, top with buttered crumbs mixed with grated cheese, and bake in 350 oven about 30 mins or until knife tested in center comes out clean.

FISH PUDDING

Combine 2 C grated raw mahimahi (or grated fish from the market) with 2 C bread crumbs. Combine 3/4 C cream or half-and-half with 6 well beaten egg yolks and add to fish mixture. Season with S&P to taste. Fold in stiffly beaten egg whites and pour into buttered mold. Steam in covered pot of simmering water for 1 hr or until silver knife comes out clean. Serve with cream sauce mixed with hard boiled eggs, mushrooms, or small shrimp.

MANFRED PIRSCHER'S COCONUT FRIED SHRIMP

Peel, clean, then butterfly 24 pieces of large shrimp and season with S&P, lemon juice, and a hint of curry.

Make a smooth batter with a 6-oz can coconut milk, 2 beaten eggs, 1 C flour, and a dash of salt.

Separately mix 1 C Panko (Japanese flour found in Oriental section) with 2 C shredded coconut. Dip shrimp into the batter so that they are well coated, then put them into the Panko-coconut mix, and press mixture on the shrimp so that they are evenly breaded. Fry in pre-heated 1/2 in oil to a golden brown. Serve with mango chutney.

You may substitute shrimp with chicken breasts cut in strips.

MARGE STROMGREN'S LOBSTER OR SHRIMP NEWBURG

Melt 2 T butter in pan and saute 1 T chopped onion, 1 t parsley or chopped chives, and 1-1/2 lbs cleaned, raw shrimp or 3 frozen rock lobster tails, cut in serving pieces, over low heat for 3 mins. Add 1 can cream of shrimp soup, 1/4 to 1/2 can milk, and 3 T sherry. Bring to a boil and simmer 5 mins. Serve over hot rice. Serves 4.

SCALLOPED OYSTERS

Grease 8 in square baking dish and sprinkle 1 C saltine cracker crumbs evenly over bottom. Cover with 1/2 pt of drained oysters, reserving liquid. Season drained oysters with S&P to taste. Add enough oyster liquid to 1 C light cream to make 2 C liquid, and pour 1/2 over oysters. Dot with 2 T butter.

Repeat layers, adding another 1/2 pt of drained oysters, the second cup of cream and oyster liquid, S&P and butter, and more cracker crumbs if you wish. Bake casserole 20-30 mins in 400 oven. Serves 7.

CLAM AND SPAGHETTI CASSEROLE

Heat 2 T butter in skillet, saute 1 large chopped onion, 1 mashed clove garlic, and 1 can sliced mushrooms. Stir in 2 10-oz cans chopped clams, 3 8-oz cans tomato sauce, and season to taste.

In large casserole, alternate layers of broken up, cooked linguini, clam sauce, and grated Parmesan cheese. Top with more cheese and 1/4 C buttered bread crumbs. Bake 30 mins in 375 oven or until browned and bubbly. Serves 6.

WELSH RAREBIT AND LOBSTER

Heat and stir 2 9-oz cans Welsh rarebit over low heat until it simmers, add 1 5-oz can lobster, drained and cubed, 1 3-oz can sliced mushrooms, and 2 T sauterne. Heat through on low heat. Spoon mixture over halved slices of toast or buttered English muffins. Serves 4.

SALMON CRUNCH PIE

Crust: cut 1/2 C butter into 1-1/2 C flour, add 1 C grated cheese and sprinkle of paprika, and mix. Put aside 1 cup of the mixture. Grease spring form tin and line with crumb mixture.

Filling: debone and flake 1 large can of salmon and combine with 1 carton sour cream, 2 T mayonnaise, 3 beaten eggs, 1/2 C grated cheese, 1 minced onion, and 1 t dill. Fill pie crust and cover with 1 C of crust mixture. Bake in 350 oven 1 hr. It's slow to settle, so allow 10 mins before cutting. Can be served hot or cold with sauce of chopped cucumber, parsley and sour cream.

SALMON SOUFFLE

Remove all bones from 1 can salmon, chop fine, and add 1/4 t salt and 1/8 t paprika.

Cook 1/2 C bread crumbs together with 1/2 C milk for 5 mins. Add 4 egg yolks and fish and 2 t lemon juice.

Beat egg whites stiff and fold in. Turn into buttered baking dish, set in pan of hot water, and bake in 350 oven till firm, about an hour.

BAKED CANNED SALMON

Drain 1 can salmon, remove skin and bones, break into good sized chunks, and lay in small greased casserole. Heat 1 T butter in skillet and saute 1 small chopped onion and 1/2 medium size green pepper until done. Add 1 can cream of mushroom soup, 1/4 C milk, blend well, and heat almost to boiling point. Pour soup mixture over salmon, cover with 1/2 C coarse bread crumbs, and sprinkle with grated Parmesan cheese. Bake in 400 oven 20 mins. Serves 4.

SALMON RING

Mix 1-1/2 C flaked fresh or canned salmon with 1 C bread crumbs. Add 3/4 C cream and unbeaten yolks of 4 eggs 1 at a time. Season with S&P, dill weed and Worcestershire Sauce, then add stiffly beaten egg whites.

Put in well-buttered ring mold, place in pan of hot water, and bake 35-40 mins or until set and silver knife comes out clean. Serve with green peas and a cream sauce or tartar sauce.

SALMON HASH

Combine de-boned can of salmon with 2 C cold mashed potatoes, 1 minced onion or 1/2 C chopped green onions, and 1/2 C chopped parsley. Season with dill weed and S&P.

Form into patties, dredge in flour, and refrigerate for at least an hour. Fry in hot oil over medium heat until brown and a nice crust has formed on bottom. Pass the catsup!

Canned salmon is a great picnic favorite, and a versatile ingredient for delicious entrees.

FRUIT

SOURSOP

This small evergreen tree seems to sag under the burden of the strange looking, heart-shaped, thick-skinned, spiny fruits about 6 to 8 in long and weighing anywhere from 1 to 6 lbs. When ripe it is still green but soft to the touch. The white cotton-like pulp is imbedded with many black seeds, and it has a bland to acid flavor.

Puree the pulp in ricer to make delicious sherbets or cool drinks. If you have the patience, pick out the seeds and use the shredded pulp in sherbets.

SIMPLE SOURSOP SURPRISE

Heat 2 C of puree and stir in 1 package strawberry or mixed fruit gelatin until dissolved. Cool to set in individual bowls and serve with cream. The strawberry has a lovely color.

SOURSOP SHERBET

Boil 2 C water and 3/4 - 1 C sugar for about 10 mins to make a syrup. Cool to lukewarm, add 2 C soursop puree, 1 T lemon juice, and 1 unbeaten egg white. Mix and pour into freezing tray.

SOURSOP MOUSSE

Soak 1/2 T unflavored gelatin in 2 T cold water and let stand until dissolved. Pour 1/3 C boiling water over gelatin and stir until dissolved. Combine with 1 C soursop puree, add 1 C sugar, and stir until dissolved. Chill, then fold in 1 C whipped cream. Refrigerate.

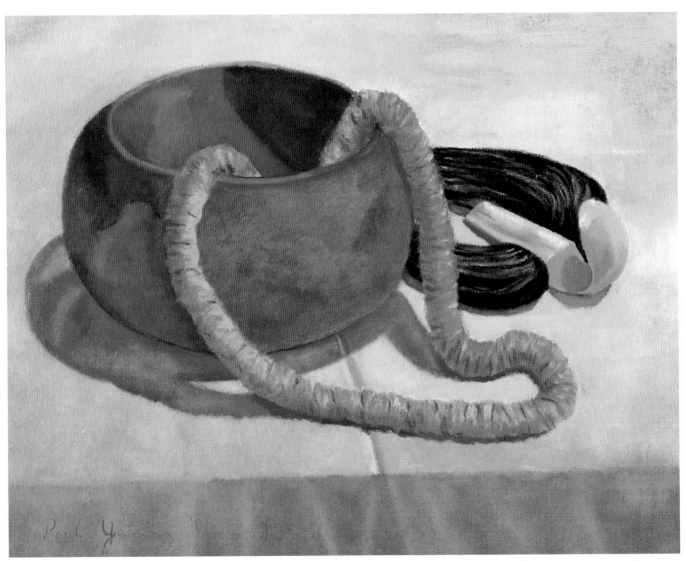

Lei Palaoa and Royal Ilima

Courtesy of Mr. Donald H. Graham, Jr.

MARCH

◆

It's March...
can Spring be far behind!

The 17th belongs to the Irish when they honor their patron, Saint Patrick, and celebrate with the "Wearin' of the Green" and appropriate victuals.

On March 26th, all the islands pay tribute to a favorite Island son who did so much for his fellow Hawaiians...Prince Jonah Kuhio Kalanianaole.

We'll go back in time to the days of yore during Prince Kuhio's time in the Islands.

AND FOR THE IRISH... STEW AND CORNED BEEF

This is a general rule of thumb for a basic stew: dredge beef cubes with flour and brown well on all sides in hot lard. It's best to do this in batches so that each piece is nicely browned.

Season with S&P and garlic powder if you desire. Cover the meat with hot water or bouillon stock, cover, and allow meat to cook slowly at a simmer until done...about 2-1/2 - 3 hrs.

45 mins before serving, add quartered onions, quartered potatoes, and cut-up carrots. Thicken the gravy at the end with a paste of flour and water.

Some people like to make the stew the day before and refrigerate it overnight before adding the vegetables. This way they can skim off any fat that has risen to the top.

Variations: toss in other vegetables...green beans, peas, cauliflower, cabbage, lima or navy beans, or canned stewed tomatoes.

Use a rich, full-bodied red wine instead of water to simmer stew.

Follow a recipe on the box of a biscuit mix and top the simmering stew with dumplings. This makes a nice change from potatoes or rice.

BURGUNDY STEW

Shake 1 lb lean stew meat in bag with flour and seasoning to coat meat. In large frying pan saute 1 quartered onion and minced bud of garlic in 2 T oil for 5 mins. Remove and add beef to brown over medium heat. Add 1-1/4 C water, 5 beef bouillon cubes, 1 t ea oregano, basil and thyme, 1 crushed bay leaf, S&P to taste, and the onions. Scrape bottom of pan drippings and turn to low heat to simmer 1 hr. Add sliced carrots, fresh mushrooms, and continue cooking 30 mins or till meat is tender. Pour in 1 C burgundy and let heat thoroughly through to serve over hot noodles. Sprinkle fresh chopped parsley over all. Serves 4.

EASY STEW

Place 2 lbs lean stew beef in casserole, sprinkle in 1 package dry onion soup mix, 1 C sherry, 1 carton of sour cream, and season to taste. Cover and bake in 350 oven 2 hrs or until meat is tender.

SIMPLE SIMON STEW

Shake 2 lbs lean stew meat in bag with flour, S&P, and garlic salt. Brown beef in oil a little at a time to brown evenly. When all browned, add 1 quartered onion, 1 chopped green pepper, 2 cloves, 1 sliced carrot, 2 minced garlic cloves, 1 40-oz can stewed tomatoes, and simmer 2-1/2 to 3 hrs or until meat is tender.

BURGUNDY OVEN STEW

Dissolve 1 envelope onion soup mix in 1-1/2 C hot water, add 1 can cream of mushroom soup, 3/4 C burgundy wine, and 2 lbs stew meat, not browned. Mix together, put in covered casserole, and cook 3 hrs in 350 oven.

FLEMISH BEER STEW

Fry 1/2 lb bacon, diced, until crisp. Set aside.

Brown 4-1/2 lbs stewing beef in fat, add 6 sliced onions, 3 large potatoes, cubed, 6 chopped carrots, 1 t thyme, 1 bay leaf, 2 T salt and dash of pepper. Pour 3 cans of beer over and bring to a boil.

Spread 3 T prepared mustard on both sides of 2 slices of de-crusted bread and place on top of stew. Cover and bake in 300 oven for 4 hrs. Remove from oven, stir bread into gravy, sprinkle with parsley and dill to taste, and add the crisp bacon. Serves 10.

SOME CELEBRATE WITH CORNED BEEF

BOILED CORNED BEEF

Cover corned beef with cold water and allow to come to a rolling boil. Drain off water, cover with water again, and let cook slowly, at a simmering temperature, until done. Allow 40 mins to 1 hr per lb for cooking. Add potatoes and carrots, cut up, the last hr, and add cabbage cut in wedge-shaped pieces the last 1/2 hr.

BAKED CORNED BEEF

Drain package of prepared corned beef with spices and lay meat on heavy aluminum foil. On both sides lay slices of 1 onion, 1 sliced orange, 1 carrot, 1 celery stick, and wrap securely. Bake in 300 oven for 3 hrs. Cook vegetables separately on top of stove...quartered onions, potatoes, and cabbage.

GLAZED CORNED BEEF

Simmer the corned beef for 3 hrs, drain, and put in pan. Pour over 1 C orange marmalade mixed with 4 t Dijon mustard, 4 T brown sugar, and be sure to coat thoroughly. Bake 30 mins in 350 oven.

BROWNED CORNED BEEF

Cook corned beef in water until done. Remove to open roasting pan and stick with whole cloves. Pour maple syrup over it and bake in 350 oven until browned.

GLAZE FOR CORNED BEEF

Dot cooked beef with cloves. Combine 3/4 C brown sugar, 1/4 t mustard, 1/4 C sherry, and 2 T corned beef stock meat has cooked in. Pour over meat and bake 45 mins at 350, basting frequently.

CORNED BEEF HASH

Combine 2 C chopped cooked corned beef, 2 C finely chopped cooked potatoes, 1 chopped onion, 1/2 C milk, and 2 eggs. Mix thoroughly and pack in greased ring mold. Bake at 350 for 45 mins.

Serve with creamed hard boiled eggs in the middle.

4 lbs of corned beef meat serves 6.

DAYS OF YORE IN HAWAII WITH PRINCE KUHIO

Kuhio's mother, Princess Kekaulike, died when her three sons were quite young, and they were adopted by her sister, Queen Kapiolani. Just before King Kalakaua's coronation ceremony, he pronounced the three nephews Princes, and they officially became a part of the royal household at Iolani Palace.

Kuhio was educated in California and then later in England. Upon his return to the Islands, he continued to live with his widowed Aunt Kapiolani in her Waikiki home, "Pualeilani", and became involved in the politics of the Islands. He married the young daughter of his aunt's friend from Kauai, who had come to live with the queen while attending school.

Prince Jonah Kuhio Kalanianaole was elected by the people of the Territory of Hawaii to represent them in Washington, D.C. as their Delegate to Congress. Prince "Cupid", as he was lovingly referred to, and his lovely wife, Kahanu, lived part-time in Washington and in their ocean front home on Kalakaua Avenue. It was a rather large 2-story cement house, and was distinguished by a lovely deep purplish-red vine named for him that grew on the fence on the street side. In front, a pier led out over the water to a good sized room that was used for entertaining.

Kahanu and Kuhio's gracious hospitality and entertaining was typical of so many kamaainas of the '20s. The homes were large with broad lanais conducive to informal living and entertaining, and the needs of the households were met by a faithful staff of men and women. The kitchen was the heart of the house and usually ruled over by an imperious male cook.

A typical kitchen of the day was large and airy and adjacent to a spacious back porch where the family had breakfast around an expandable table, bunches of ripening bananas were hung, other fruits were brought in to ripen and the trusty ice box stood.

In the middle of the kitchen sat a good sized zinc-topped or wooden table that was kept scrubbed to a high patina. Stools kept under the table could be easily brought out when having late snacks. A meat grinder could be quickly and securely fastened to the table, or covered with a thick padding the table top could be converted into a super-size ironing board to handle the large cut-work linen tablecloths.

Original sinks were made of zinc with drains made of the same material or wood until replaced with a standard four-legged white tile sink. Even today, many kamaainas refer to that area as "the zinc."

At the end of one drain hung an erstwhile kerosene can for slops which was emptied, cleaned, and replaced every other day by the "slop man." The wood-burning stove or large gas or electric stove took up one end of the kitchen. There were at least six burners, and on the ledge above were jars of Hawaiian salt, chili pepper water, soy, Crisco, a box of big matches and a glass jar containing all the burned ones. Three ovens and a good-size warmer on top served most purposes.

The old-fashioned wooden ice box was usually on the back porch, purely for utilitarian reasons. The dripping water from the thawing block of ice was funneled down into a large drip pan beneath the ice box that had to be emptied at least once a day. Later, a system of pipes carried the flow outside into the yard, but this had to be cleaned of the "limu" that abounded. Also it was more convenient for the ice man and milk man. The ice box had three doors. The ice compartment took up three-quarters of the space on the left, leaving a little space beneath for small things, but the milk and butter and any setting gelatin were always placed immediately around or on top of the block of ice. The other side of the box contained shelves of wire racks for food that was quickly consumed, so there was never much clutter. However, there was always a supply of jars containing different types of limu, kukui nut, opihis, and large bowls of poi which had been left on the counters to sour.

Extra ice had to be ordered whenever there was ice cream to be made, and this was an exciting production that brought in help from all sides, especially when the blade was removed! Everyone took a turn at cranking the handle that churned the ice cream container surrounded by crushed ice and Hawaiian salt.

Nearby stood a screened food safe with its four legs in small cans of water so the ants couldn't get at the stored jars of sugar, flour, butter, jelly, crackers, etc.

The milk man added to the flow of traffic. He placed the glass bottles of rich milk next to the block of ice and picked up the empty ones. In those days, the neck of the bottle was filled with a very thick, yellow cream which had to be scooped out before the milk could even be shaken or poured.

The faithful "vegetable man" arrived at the kitchen door twice a week in his rattle-trap vending truck laden with fresh fruits and vegetables, various and sundry staples, bread, and some meat and fresh fish on occasion. The kids of the household could always be counted on to purchase 5-cent bags of crack seed and snitch stray stems of watercress. But it was Cook-san who was entrusted with buying for the family, and was counted on to drive a hard bargain, too.

The large pantry between the dining room and kitchen contained glass cupboards for the "good" china and crystal, a small sink for rinsing off glasses and polishing silver, and a heavy safe for silver.

The storeroom resembled the shelves of a mini-mart, with its private reserve of home-made jams, jellies, pickles, chutney, pickled onions, coffee beans with the grinder nearby, and an ample supply of canned milk, soda water, and assorted canned goods.

When Kuhio and Kahanu had visiting mainland friends, they usually stayed either at the Moana Hotel down the road or downtown at either the Alexander Young Hotel or the Blaisdell Hotel. However, there were many small family-type hotels in quiet neighborhoods scattered around the city. The main building was usually an old converted mansion, with comfortable cottages nestled in the surrounding tropical gardens. Some even had swimming tanks for the guests' enjoyment. These small hotels were occupied mostly by local residents and some transient visitors, and operated on the American plan which included three excellent meals a day, all for $3 and up. Street cars with motormen and conductors ran along tracks in the main streets leading into town and to Waikiki, Kalihi and the valleys.

One such hostelry, The Donna Hotel, was opened by Mrs. Charles Justin McCarthy after her husband ended his term as governor of the Territory of Hawaii and they had returned to their large home on Beretania St.

The rooms were simply furnished, clean, and always cool. The high-ceilinged public rooms featured comfortable wicker furniture, a game table, numerous potted palms and ferns, and a small but interesting library of books and magazines. The dining room had tables for as many as eighty guests, and the floors throughout were covered with lauhala mats. The guest rooms had a basin in one corner of the room, a comfortable chair, desk, and a bed covered with a white cotton counterpane. Suspended from the ceiling over the bed hung a mosquito net gathered in a large loop under the hoop. At night this was undone and securely tucked under the mattress for protection from pesky mosquitos.

Guests at The Donna Hotel were especially fortunate. Mrs. McCarthy was a famous Island cook, and her recipes and menus were referred to as the "Kitchen Bible." Having been a gracious hostess for the Governor at Washington Place, she assumed her role at the hotel as a natural one.

Her recipes and others are so typical of that era and almost always took considerable time to prepare. However, Island hostesses in those days never begrudged the time spent in the kitchen, especially if they had a dependable cook!

CHOP SUEY

Cut 2 lbs fresh pork, 1 lb round steak, and 1 C ham in thin strips. Fry in peanut oil till done and then add 1 sliced Chinese cabbage, 1 t salt, 1/4 t black pepper, 1 t chopped ginger root, 1 large sliced onion, 1 minced clove garlic, 2 carrots cut in thin strips, sliced string beans, sliced bamboo shoots, Chinese peas, and dry mushrooms which have been soaked in water and cut in strips. Stir-fry quickly, as the vegetables must be crisp, not soft.

Add soy and a sprinkle of sugar to taste, and when done, add bean sprouts, cook just a few minutes, then add chopped green onions and chives.

BAKED CHICKEN, RICE, AND ALMONDS

Gently boil a 5 lb chicken (whole) adding to the water a few slices of onion, a stalk of celery, and a slice of carrot. Add salt during the last hour of cooking. Let chicken cool in the broth. When cool, cut meat in fairly large pieces, using scissors.

Wash 1 C rice, add 1-1/4 C of the chicken broth, and cook 10 mins.

Make a medium thick white sauce using 1/4 C butter, 1/4 C flour, 1 C milk, and 1 C cream or evaporated milk. Season to taste.

Have ready 1 medium can mushrooms, drained, 1 small can pimento, chopped and drained, and 1 C blanched chopped almonds.

Into a large buttered casserole, put first a layer of rice, then a layer of chicken, then a layer of white sauce, and sprinkle with pimento, almonds, and mushrooms. Repeat until all ingredients are used, ending with rice. Add a little more chicken broth if the mixture does not seem moist enough.

Cover with buttered cracker crumbs and bake in 375 oven for 45 to 60 mins. If desired, broth may be thickened with flour and used for gravy.

COCKTAIL DRESSING

Use for fresh oysters, clams, opihi, alligator pears, papaya, etc.

Combine 1 part Worcestershire Sauce, 2 parts catsup, 1 part vinegar (or 2 parts lemon juice), a dash of tabasco, some sugar, and S&P to taste. Place on ice till cold.

The proper amount of the different ingredients to use can only be learned with practice.

COCONUT FRITTERS

Cook until thick: 1 qt milk, 1/4 C cornstarch, 2 T sugar, and 1 grated coconut. Pour into pan to cool, cut in squares, dip in bread crumbs, and cook in deep fat. Serve with maple or coconut syrup.

FISH CHOWDER

Cut 2 lbs firm white fish into small pieces, put in cold water with bones, and boil until cooked. Cut 3 medium potatoes into cubes and boil to cook. Fry up a bit of sliced bacon or salt pork and add 2 sliced onions. Cook until limp. De-bone fish and return to pot. Add pork and onion and 1 pt milk or cream. Season with 1/2 T salt and 1/2 t pepper, simmer, and serve piping hot with saloon pilots.

CLAM SOUFFLE

Fry 1 good size onion, chopped, in a little butter. Add 1 heaping T flour, 1/2 C milk, 1 tin minced clams, and salt to taste. Remove from stove and add 3 beaten eggs and 2 chopped pimentos. Bake in buttered casserole until brown and set in 350 oven.

LEMON PUDDING

Grate 3 lemons; add the juice and rind to 3/4 C sugar.

Soak 1 T gelatin in a little cold water and add to juice when soft. Put all in double boiler and add 7 egg yolks beaten well with 3/4 C sugar. Cook until it thickens, then fold in 7 well beaten egg whites. Refrigerate to set and serve with whipped cream.

PRUNE SOUFFLE

Strain 2 lbs cooked, mashed prunes, add 5 T sugar and 1 T vanilla. Place in oven until hot. Beat 4 egg whites until stiff and beat into prunes. Bake in buttered dish about 15 mins. Serve with whipped cream.

ONO PRUNE CAKE

Cook 2 C dried prunes in water in which they were soaked overnight, and when soft remove the stones and mash the prunes to a pulp.

Combine 4 C flour with 1 t ea cinnamon, nutmeg, and cloves.

Liquify 1 t baking soda with a little water.

Cream 1 C butter, add 1 C sugar a little at a time, and continue until all the sugar is used, cream until soft. Add the 5 egg yolks and 1 whole egg which have been beaten together a little while. Then add flour mixture alternately with mashed prunes. If the batter is not soft enough to drop easily from a spoon, add more prune juice or water. Lastly, add the baking soda mixed with water. Turn into greased cake pans and bake in 350 oven 25 mins.

Frosting: use the 5 whites of the eggs beaten until stiff but not dry, then add enough sugar to make it thick and fluffy. A little of the mashed prunes may be added to the frosting if desired. Add any flavoring desired. Pour some frosting between layers and then cover cake completely with the frosting.

THE DONNA HOTEL PUMPKIN PIE

Mix 2 C mashed pumpkin, 2 C milk, 1 C brown sugar, 1 T molasses, 2 beaten eggs, 1/2 t ea cinnamon, salt, ginger, and nutmeg. Pour into prepared pie crust, bake in 375 oven 1 hr or until silver knife comes out clean. Double recipe makes 3 pies.

LIGHT FRUIT CAKE

Cream 3/4 C butter, add 1 C sugar, and beat until really fluffy. Add 4 eggs, 2 C flour sifted with 1/2 t baking soda and 1 t nutmeg. Add 1-1/2 C ea seedless raisins and chopped walnuts, 1/4 lb candied cherries or candied pineapple, chopped, and the grated rind of 1 lemon. Mix well and bake in 300 degree oven about 1 hr.

DATE BARS

Mix 3/4 C flour, 1 t baking powder, 1 C sugar, and 1/4 t salt.

Add 1 C ea chopped dates and walnuts and fold in 2 well beaten eggs. Spread in greased pan 1/2 in thick and bake in 350 oven until done.

APPLE UPSIDE DOWN CAKE

Butter generously an 8-in square pan. Slice 4 medium tart apples thinly until pan is half full. Cover with 1 t cinnamon and 1 C sugar.

Batter: Sift 1 C flour with 1 t baking powder, add 1 C sugar and 1/4 t salt.

Heat 1/2 C milk with 1 T butter and when scalding hot, pour over 2 well beaten eggs and beat until very light. Add to flour mixture. Add 1 t flavoring and mix well. Pour over apples and bake 45 mins at 350. Serve warm with whipped cream.

GRAHAM CRACKER CRUST

Mix 1-1/2 C crushed graham crackers, 1/3 C powdered sugar, 1/2 C melted butter, and pat into pie pan. Bake 5 mins.

CHOCOLATE WAFER CRUST

Combine 20 chocolate wafers (or 1-1/4 C chocolate wafer crumbs) with 1/3 C melted butter and pat into pie pan. Bake 10 mins and fill with favorite creamy filling.

GREEN MAYONNAISE

In saucepan combine 4 C washed and drained spinach leaves and 1 C each parsley sprigs and watercress sprigs. Cover with water, add 1 t salt, and simmer 2 min. Drain thoroughly and puree greens with 1 T lemon juice. Blend well with 1 C mayonnaise and chill. Serve with sliced avocado and shrimp or crab salad. Garnish with sprigs of watercress.

NOTES

Mangoes   *Courtesy of Dr. William L. Theobald*

APRIL

◆

It's April and Spring is in the air!
Beware the pranksters
on the first!

The actual date of Easter Sunday varies from year to year, but it can't be earlier than March 22nd or later than April 25th. So this is generally the month we prepare for the promised joys of Easter.

Look for kumquats, loquats, mangoes, and if you find a tree...mulberries.

EASTER FARE: LAMB, HAM AND ACCOMPANIMENTS

In the Christian adult world, Easter Sunday is a time for rejoicing and giving thanks; to the very young, it's visions of Easter bunnies hopping to their doors dispensing fancy baskets of colored eggs and candies; and to the young at heart, Easter brings out an extra ribbon here, a bow there, and a bonnet festooned with bright spring flowers for the Easter Parade.

To young and old alike, the holiday spirit means remembering with spring bouquets and entertaining family and friends with a very special meal. Traditionally, it's either Roast Leg of Lamb or a "picture book" Baked Ham. However, it could simply be a Sunday Breakfast after church with something extra special that you have prepared ahead of time.

Whatever you have, set a joyous mood for your Easter brunch, lunch or dinner. Cover your table with a bright flowered or yellow tablecloth with matching napkins, and place a large Easter basket filled with cellophane grass, dyed eggs, chocolate bunnies and yellow chicks, or mixed spring flowers in the center.

LAMB

Roast leg of lamb flavored with garlic and fresh rosemary is the favorite, but mint, basil, lemon, Worcestershire Sauce, and curry are most compatible, too!

ROAST LEG OF LAMB

Make small slits in a 6-7 lb leg of lamb and insert garlic slivers evenly in the leg, rub all over with lemon juice, and pat rosemary, thyme, and S&P evenly over surface.

Place in roasting pan in 400 oven for 10 mins, reduce heat to 350, and roast for 1-1/2 hrs for medium rare. Let stand 10 mins before carving.

Add quartered potatoes and onions the last hr and turn to brown evenly.

ROAST LEG OF LAMB

For a 6-7 lb leg of lamb, insert sharp knife under meat's surface, slit about 7-in long openings, and press slivers of garlic into each pocket. Combine S&P to taste, 1/2 t each thyme and oregano, 1/4 t paprika, and rub well into lamb.

On bottom of roasting pan spread 1 thinly sliced onion, 1 chopped rib of celery, 1 coarsely chopped carrot, and set leg on top. Baste with combination of 1/2 C dry white wine and 1 C beef broth.

Bake at 350 for 20 to 25 mins per lb or until done to your preference. Remove roast, keep warm, spoon off as much fat as possible from pan juices, cook juices and vegetables over high heat, adjust seasoning, strain into heated gravy boat, and serve with sliced lamb.

MARINATED LAMB

Combine 1 C plain yogurt, 1 T each oil and soy, 1/2 t dry mustard, dash of rosemary, and S&P. Place 6-7 lb lamb on large sheet of tin foil, brush thoroughly with marinade, wrap carefully, seal securely, and place in refrigerator for 4-7 days.

After 3 days, open package, cut slits in lamb and insert as many slivers of garlic as your taste dictates, and return to refrigerator. To bake, unwrap and scrape off sauce, place lamb in roasting pan, add 1 C white wine, and roast at 350 for 10 mins. Reduce heat to 300 and continue cooking 15 mins per lb. Remove from oven and allow roast to sit for 20 mins before carving. Remove fat from juices.

LOUISE JUDD'S MARINADE
FOR LEG OF LAMB

Marinate overnight in a mixture of half brandy and half port. Cut slits in meat and insert fresh rosemary before marinating. Roast at 200 1 hr per lb, basting occasionally with marinade.

ROSEMARY'S LAMB MARINADE

Combine in blender container: 1 lg clove garlic, crushed, 4 chopped green onions, juice of 2 lemons, 1-1/2 t salt, 1 t ground black pepper, 1/2 C parsley, 4 crushed bay leaves, 1/2 C white wine, and 1/2 C soy.

Blend and gradually add 1/2 C olive oil to make an emulsion, and marinate lamb overnight.

Brown lamb quickly with top heat, then bake at 350 about 45 mins to 1 hr.

GERRY'S SPIRITED MINT LAMB

Combine 1 C each creme de menthe and chopped onions, 2 cloves minced garlic, 1 t salt, and 1/4 t pepper. Pierce leg of lamb all over with a skewer or ice pick and place in a shallow dish or plastic bag. Pour marinade over, cover or seal, and place in refrigerator 24 hrs or more, turning often.

Drain, save marinade, and put lamb in roasting pan. Bake at 325 for 1-1/2 to 2 hrs. Baste with marinade during roasting, adding water if too dry.

While roast sits, make gravy by adding 1/2 C of marinade to pan juices, 1 C heavy cream, 2 T butter, and 2 T cornstarch mixed with water, and stir into gravy. Cook and check seasoning. Serve with lamb.

STEPHEN REED'S MINT SAUCE

Heat 3 T water, dissolve 1-1/2 T sugar in it, and cool. Add 1/3 C finely chopped mint leaves and 1/2 C vinegar. Best made 1/2 hr before serving. Makes 1 C.

TASTY LAMB SHANK CASSEROLE

Trim fat from 6 lamb shanks, rub with garlic cloves, and roll in mixture of 1/4 C flour, 2 t salt, and 1 t paprika.

Add 2 T oil to skillet and brown shanks evenly in sizzling oil. Lay shanks in a large casserole.

Into skillet stir 1/2 C lemon juice to loosen browned drippings, add 1/2 C ea dry white wine and chicken broth, and pour over shanks. Sprinkle 2 T grated lemon rind over and add 1 small bay leaf and 4 peppercorns.

Cover and bake 1 hr in 350 oven. Add 1 can small whole onions, small new potatoes, and 2 carrots, sliced. Continue baking, covered, 45 mins to an hr longer. When cooked, take out the shanks, remove meat from bones, and return large chunks to casserole.

BAKED LAMB SHANKS

Sprinkle 4 lamb shanks with S&P and place in a roasting pan.

Combine 1 can tomatoes, 1/2 C burgundy, claret, or other red table wine, 1 C chopped celery, 1/2 C chopped onion, 2 minced garlic buds, and dash of rosemary or marjoram.

Heat mixture to simmering and pour over lamb. Bake uncovered in 375 oven for 2 to 2-1/2 hrs or until meat is tender. Turn shanks occasionally during cooking and baste with the sauce. Serves 4.

CRUSTY POTATO CUPS

Peel and coarsely shred 3 medium size potatoes into a bowl of water. When all shredded, lift out and dry thoroughly. Then mix with minced medium size onion, 1-1/4 C shredded Swiss cheese, S&P, and 1/4 t nutmeg until well blended.

Generously butter 12 muffin cups, sprinkle paprika lightly over butter, and press the potato mixture evenly into each cup. Bake uncovered in 450 oven for 45 mins or until edges are well browned and potato is no longer moist in center. Remove from oven and let cool about 5 mins. Loosen edges with a knife, lift out potato cups, and invert each onto a slice of tomato. Serve at once. Pass sour cream to spoon over.

POTATOES AU GRATIN

Scald 1-1/2 C milk, cool briefly, and pour into mixing bowl. Combine with 1 beaten egg, 1-1/2 lbs potatoes which have been peeled and thinly sliced, 1/2 C grated Swiss cheese, a pinch of nutmeg, and S&P to taste. Mix the ingredients thoroughly.

Pour the mixture into heavy casserole which has been rubbed with garlic and well buttered. Sprinkle the top with grated Swiss cheese and dot evenly with 3 T butter. Bake in 350 oven for about 45 mins, or until the potatoes are cooked through. Serve from the casserole.

POTATO WEDGES

Scrub 6 medium potatoes and cut in half lengthwise, then cut in wedges. Boil wedges for 5 mins in salted water, drain, and pat dry. Spread wedges in single layer on lightly greased baking sheet, sprinkle with 3 T oil, 1/2 t ea salt, oregano, thyme, and dashes of black pepper and cayenne.

Bake at 425 for about 15 mins. Sprinkle with 1/2 C grated Parmesan Cheese and 2 T grated cheddar cheese and bake for another 10 to 12 mins, or until potatoes are golden brown and cheeses are melted.

Any type of potato goes well with lamb.

Cook new potatoes in rapidly boiling water. When cooked, drain water immediately and put uncovered saucepan back on low heat, shaking the pan gently to dry out the potatoes quickly. Add butter and chopped parsley.

When making mashed potatoes, add milk or light cream that has been heated to make mixture smooth and fluffy, then add butter and S&P.

SPOON BREAD
will surprise them!

Add 1 C cornmeal to 2 C scalded milk, stirring constantly till smooth. When mixture is lukewarm, add 3 well beaten egg yolks, beating the while, and 1 t salt and 2 t baking powder.

Fold in 3 stiffly beaten egg whites. Pour into greased casserole 4 or 5 in deep and bake at 375 for about 35 mins. Serves 6 to 8.

A cheese version has 1 additional egg and includes 1/4 C melted butter and 1-1/2 C shredded cheddar.

GLAZED PAPAYA QUARTERS
is a natural with lamb.

In a small pan, combine 1/4 C butter or margarine, 1 t ea ground ginger and ground coriander, and 1/4 t curry powder. Cook over low heat until bubbly. Stir in 2 T ea honey and lime juice.

Cut 2 papayas (unpeeled) lengthwise in quarters, remove seeds, and set in a baking pan, cut side up. Brush butter mixture over the fruit. Bake in 325 oven, basting occasionally, about 25 mins or until hot. Pour any remaining mixture into papaya cavities, then serve with meat. Serves 8.

SPINACH SURPRISE

Cook 3 packages frozen chopped spinach according to directions, drain well. Melt 1/2 C butter and 1 C creamed cheese over low heat, stirring until smooth, then add 2/3 T lemon juice. Add spinach to cheese sauce and mix thoroughly. Add S&P to taste.

Place 1 jar artichoke hearts that have been cut in thirds in bottom of buttered 1-1/2 qt casserole. Cover artichokes with spinach mixture, top with buttered bread crumbs, and bake at 350 for 30 mins.

HAM

From an 1894 cookbook comes this recipe for serving ham.

Boil a 10-12 lb ham slowly for 3 hrs, strip off the skin, take a sharp knife and shave off the outer surface very thin, and if quite fat, take off a little. Spread over the fat part a thin coating of brown sugar, then put the ham in a baking pan with 1/2 pt of white wine to roast 1/2 hr. Baste often, taking care that the juices do not scorch, and it will make nice gravy. Sliver very thin, whether served hot or cold.

GLAZED FRESH HAM

Remove ham skin and trim excess fat from a 10 lb ham, rub with S&P, and let stand at room temperature for 1 hr. Place in roasting pan in 400 oven for 30 mins, reduce to 325, and roast for 25 mins per lb. This should take about 4 hrs.

Baste every 20 mins with guava juice and pan drippings. About 1/2 hr before finished, remove ham from oven, gash the fat in diamond pattern, and stick cloves in slits. Spread with paste of guava juice, brown sugar, and mustard to taste, and baste to glaze well.

You may want to secure pineapple slices on ham and fill center with red cherries.

BAKED HAM

Peel the skin of 16 lb pre-cooked smoked ham with bone, trim the fat, and score with sharp knife. Place ham on foil-lined baking pan, insert whole cloves in cuts of fat. Combine 1/4 C mustard with 1 C packed dark brown sugar and coat ham. Pour 2 C guava or pineapple juice in pan and baste occasionally for 2 hrs in 350 oven. Check so pan isn't scorching.

ALICE MEIDEROS'
SPECIAL HAM MARINADE

Alice Meideros has her own special marinade for her Easter ham. It can either be for a canned or 4 lb Farmer John ham.

Place ham in pan and make holes in the meat with either a very sharp knife or ice pick so the juices will seep down into the meat. Spread over a coating of brown sugar, minced garlic and onions to taste, prepared mustard, dust with either powdered cloves or stick with whole cloves, and pour over all a can of orange exchange base and small can crushed pineapple.

Cover and marinate for 3 days in refrigerator, turning once or twice. Add water to pan so not to scorch glaze and bake in 250-300 oven for 4 hrs. Test meat to see that it is done well.

DRUNKEN HAM

Score boiled or canned ham, pour bourbon on and into cuts. Combine 2 C brown sugar and 1 T dry mustard with a little bourbon to form paste, and pat on ham. Insert whole cloves in slits. Bake in 450 oven to brown fat to a golden brown.

CRANBERRY-BURGUNDY GLAZED HAM

Place a 10-14 lb bone-in fully cooked ham fat side up in shallow pan, score fat in diamond pattern, and stud with cloves. Bake 2-1/2 - 3 hrs in 325 oven.

In a saucepan combine 1 can whole cranberry sauce, 1 C brown sugar, 1/2 C burgundy, 2 t prepared mustard, and simmer 5 mins.

Last 30 min of baking, spoon 1/2 the glaze over ham and serve remaining glaze as sauce.

RAISIN SAUCE FOR HAM

Cook 1 C sugar and 1/2 C water 5 mins. Add 1 C raisins, seedless or cut in pieces, 2 T butter, 3 T vinegar, 1 jar fruit jelly, 1/2 T Worcestershire Sauce, 1/2 t salt, 1/8 t pepper, 1/4 t clove, and dash of mace. Cook until jelly dissolves...about 20-30 mins.

Serve with slices of ham at table.

BAKED BEANS are a natural with ham.

Fry up 1 Portuguese sausage, sliced, with 1 diced onion and 1 clove minced garlic, and combine with 2 1-lb 12-oz cans pork and beans, 1/2 C brown sugar, 2 T molasses, 2/3 C catsup, and 1 t dry mustard in a bean pot. Bake 2 hrs uncovered in 325 oven.

Top with slices of lemon if you so desire.

LIMA BEAN CASSEROLE
FROM THE FILES OF PHOEBE PUMMEL

Combine and mix well 2 or 3 cans (8-oz) lima beans, 1 chopped onion, 1 can condensed tomato soup, 3/4 C brown sugar, 1 t mustard, and dash of catsup. Pour into casserole, lay strips of bacon on top or combine sliced Portuguese sausage with beans, and bake in 350 oven for 2-3 hrs.

NOODLES ALFREDO

Cook 1 lb medium egg noodles according to directions on package and drain well. Melt 1/2 lb butter or oleo in large skillet, add noodles, and toss gently. Add 2 C grated Parmesan cheese and toss to distribute evenly. Slowly pour in 1/2 C heavy cream at room temperature and toss to blend. Sprinkle with pepper and serve hot in casserole. Serves 6 to 8.

NOODLES AND CHEESE

Put 1 5-oz package egg noodles into 2 qts boiling water with salt and let boil 20 mins or until tender. Drain and blanch with cold water. Place noodles in buttered baking dish, add 1/4 lb grated American cheese, mix well, add 1 pt half-and-half, S&P to taste, and bake in 350 oven 1 hr or until all liquid is absorbed.

MACARONI AND CHEESE

Cook 1 package 8 or 9 oz macaroni according to directions. Melt 1/4 C butter or margarine in small heavy saucepan, stir in 1/4 C flour, and blend in 2 C milk with wire whisk. Bring slowly to boiling point, stirring constantly. Cook 2 mins and season with S&P to taste.

Place half the macaroni in ungreased 2 qt casserole, sprinkle with 2 T grated onion and 1-1/4 C grated sharp cheddar cheese. Repeat layer and pour the white sauce over the top. Dot with butter and more cheese and bake in 350 oven 30 mins covered. Remove cover and bake 15 mins more. Serves 6-8.

SWEET POTATO BISCUITS

Season 3/4 C mashed sweet potatoes with 1 T brown sugar and S&P to taste. Stir in 1/4 C melted butter, 1/3 C milk, and 1/3 C bourbon.

Toss 1-1/4 C flour with 2-1/2 t baking powder and 1 t salt. Gradually work into potato mixture and pat dough 1/2 in thick on waxed paper. Cut into small rounds and bake at 450 about 15 mins or until biscuits are golden brown and crusty.

POLENTA is a great discovery! As a starch it's generally more interesting than rice or potatoes and more flavorful than pasta!

Add 2 C of yellow cornmeal gradually into 6 or 7 C salted simmering water and stir constantly about 20 mins. It is done when it comes away from the side of the pot.

Or cook the cornmeal in chicken stock with a little cream.

Allow polenta to cool and harden after pouring into dish. Slice into serving pieces and fry in a skillet with sizzling oil until golden brown on each side.

For a more flavorful dish, add grated Parmesan cheese before cooling.

EASTER CASSEROLES

If you are only planning a simple breakfast or brunch, the following might be something you can prepare the day before and simply warm and serve with a minimum of trouble.

CREAMED CHIP BEEF

Cook 2 stalks chopped celery and 1 chopped onion in 1/4 C margarine, stir in 3 T flour over low heat for 3 mins. Add 2 C scalded milk and cook until thickened. Add a 5-oz jar of chip beef, shredded and rinsed, and add 1/2 C thawed peas, 4 hard-boiled eggs, coarsely chopped, and 1 C chopped mushrooms.

Check for seasoning as chip beef tends to be salty, correct seasoning, and keep warm in casserole. Serve over de-crusted and halved slices of toast, and sprinkle with chopped parsley.

Or pour into halved and de-seeded papaya shells, top with buttered bread crumbs, and bake in 350 oven until bubbly hot.

CREAMY HAM CASSEROLE

Melt 1/4 C butter, stir in 1/3 C flour, add 1 C milk, and cook, stirring until mixture thickens. Add 1 C sharp cubed cheddar cheese and 1/2 C sour cream, stirring until cheese melts. Then combine with 2 C cooked cubed ham and 1 can sliced and drained mushrooms. Turn into casserole, top with buttered bread crumbs, and bake uncovered for 40 mins in 350 oven. Serves 6.

HAM LOAF

Preheat oven to 350.

Combine 1 C each diced ham, cooked macaroni, soft bread crumbs, shredded cheddar cheese and light cream, 1 large onion, chopped, 1 t chopped parsley, 1/3 C melted butter and 3 well beaten eggs. Mix well and turn into ungreased loaf pan. Bake uncovered in pan of water 1 hour.

Sauce: Combine 1 can cream of mushroom soup with 1 can sliced mushrooms, drained, and 1/2 C light cream. Heat while stirring and serve to pour over ham loaf.

FRUIT

KUMQUATS LOQUATS MANGOES MULBERRIES

This is the season for kumquats, loquats, mangoes, and mulberries!

KUMQUATS

This fruit rates high on the list of more exotic citrus found in the Islands. This small, orange-like fruit was brought to the islands before 1880 from China, but still isn't raised commercially or usually found in markets. It depends on the generosity of friends.

Not only are preserved kumquats delicious in a variety of dishes, the left-over juice in the pot can be bottled and used as syrup over ice cream, in fruit cocktails, and simply delicious when used to baste a pork roast.

PRESERVED WHOLE KUMQUATS

Clean and punch 1-1/2 lbs of kumquats in 4 places with needle and combine with 1 pt water, 1 C sugar, juice of a lime, and grated ginger to taste. Simmer until liquid becomes thick and translucent. Jar in sterilized jars.

KUMQUAT JAM

Wash fruit, cut in half crosswise, squirt out seeds, and juice through strainer, combine juice with fruit shells, and chop coarsely in food processor. For 3 C pulp, add 3/4 C water and 5 C sugar. Let it come to a rolling boil, turn down heat, and cook slowly, stirring occasionally until it sheets from the spoon. Jar in sterilized jars.

KUMQUAT PRESERVE

Sprinkle 4 C kumquats with 1 T baking soda, pour over boiling water to cover, steep 2 min, and pour off water. Cook with water to cover for 25 mins and drain. Stick kumquats with whole cloves.

Combine 3 C sugar with 3 C water and 1 C white corn syrup, bring to a boil, and gently simmer kumquats in mixture with sliced ginger to taste for about 40 mins or until glossy and transparent. Seal in sterilized jars.

LOQUATS

This is not to be confused with the kumquat. The yellow egg-shaped fruit has a white to yellow-orange flesh, a bit like apricots with a perfumed taste.

Discard the 3 or 4 large brown seeds, peel, slice, and mix with seedless grapes or other fruits for salad or fruit cups.

Stew the fruit with slices of preserved ginger and water to cover, and serve with cream or make into pies. If you leave the pits in while stewing, it has a rather almond-like taste.

LOQUAT JAM

Wash, peel, and chop fine 1 lb loquats. Combine 1-1/2 C sugar with 1 C water and 1/4 C lemon juice, add fruit, and cook, stirring occasionally until it sheets from the spoon. Pour into sterilized jars.

MANGOES

Depending on climatic conditions, mangoes should be available from this month through September and October. This fruit is rich in Vitamin A and C, and the fresh, ripe fruit can be peeled and eaten as is or served in drinks, fruit salads, cocktails, baked, or frozen in desserts, and makes beautiful preserves.

FREEZING MANGOES

It's best to freeze mangoes in small containers, as they should be thawed quickly for best results. It's even a good idea to add them to your fruit cocktail while still slightly frozen.

To freeze mangoes, wash, peel, and slice large cheeks away from each side of the seed. Freeze these slices whole, sliced smaller, or diced. (The stem area tends to be tougher and the seed flesh is pithy.)

PACKING IN SYRUP

Bring 1-1/2 C sugar (depending on sweetness of fruit) and 2 C water to a boil, cool, pour into cartons, slice in the mangoes, and freeze.

Some prefer to simply pour over thawed frozen orange juice and freeze.

SUGAR PACK

Slice desired mangoes into bowl, sprinkle with sugar (1 part sugar to 8 or 10 parts fruit), and gently mix with fruit until sugar is dissolved. Pour into Ziploc bags or containers and freeze.

MANGO SAUCE

It's better to use mature green mangoes (before they have any color) for sauce, as these don't tend to be stringy. Peel and slice mangoes in slivers into a pot with a large flat bottom so slivers are spread out.

Add just enough water so the mixture will steam but not burn: about 8-10 C mangoes to 1-1/2 C water. Stir over medium to low heat until soft like apple sauce. Mash, add 3 C brown or white sugar according to sweetness, and continue cooking until sugar is dissolved. Jar and keep refrigerated.

MANGO CHUTNEY

Green common mangoes are still the best for chutney. However, if desperate, other varieties, mainly Hayden, may be used.

Wash, peel, and slice about 50 common mangoes (green to barely half-ripe), sprinkle generously with Hawaiian salt, and let stand overnight or at least for 3 hrs.

You'll need a huge pot to boil 5 lbs of sugar with 1 qt vinegar until syrupy, about 20 minutes. Drain half the mangoes and add to syrup, and continue cooking another 30 mins.

Add 3 large chopped onions, 6 chopped garlic cloves, 1/2 C grated or finely sliced fresh ginger, 1 17-oz jar preserved sliced ginger plus the juice, 2 1-lb cartons glazed fruit cake mix, 1 #3 can pitted apricots, 1 15-oz box seedless raisins, 4 T salt, 1 t ea ginger, cinnamon, and allspice.

Stir well, add remaining mangoes, and check seasoning. Continue cooking over medium to low heat for about 1-1/2 hrs, but keep stirring so chutney doesn't burn or stick to bottom.

If you like it hot, add chopped de-seeded Hawaiian chili peppers to taste or hang a bag of 6 red peppers in the pot and remove when chutney is finished.

Pour into sterile jars, cover with paraffin, and label with date. Chutney improves with age. Just a tip: make small and medium size jars if possible. They make great gifts!

MANGO JAM

Combine 4 C water with 12 C ripe mango slices and cook until tender. Press mixture through sieve, add 6 C sugar (or to taste), and simmer over medium heat, stirring frequently for about 20 mins or until mixture reaches jam consistency. Pour into sterile jars and seal with paraffin.

MANGO MARMALADE

Cook 4 C diced mangoes at low heat about 25 mins or until mushy and reduced to about 3 cups. (Do not add water.) Add 2 T lemon juice, 1/4 C slivered lemon rind and pulp, and 3 C sugar. Boil rapidly, stirring constantly, for about 10 mins or until mixture looks clear and lemon slivers are translucent.

Pour into sterilized dry jars and seal immediately. Store in dark place to preserve colors.

RAY'S SUPER MANGO BREAD

Stir 2 C flour, 2 t ea baking soda and cinnamon, 1-1/2 C sugar, and 1/2 t salt. Combine 3/4 C salad oil, 3 lightly beaten eggs, 2 C diced ripe mangoes, 1 t vanilla extract, 1/2 C ea chopped walnuts, shredded coconut, and raisins, and combine with dry ingredients.

Lightly butter or grease 4 2-1/2x5 in loaf pans or 2 large loaf pans, and pour in the batter to 3/4 in full. Allow to stand 20 mins and bake 55 mins or 1 hr and 5 mins in 350 oven. This is a special treat!

For a tasty **MANGO SALAD**, combine diced Pirie mangoes with chopped crispy watercress and toss with your favorite dressing.

MANGO CAKE

Combine 1-1/2 C sugar and 1/2 C oil and mix well. Add 3 eggs one at a time and continue mixing. Combine 2 C flour, 1 t ea baking powder, baking soda and cinnamon, 1/4 t salt, and blend in well. Add 2 C shredded half-ripe mangoes and 1/2 C chopped nuts. Mix well, pour into 13x9x2 in greased pan, and bake 55 mins in 350 oven. Remove from oven and sprinkle with powdered sugar. Cake should be moist and fluffy.

MANGO AU CREME BRULEE

Peel and cube mangoes, arrange in baking dish, and spoon a carton of thick sour cream over. Smooth with spatula and refrigerate.

Just before serving, add a 1/2 in layer of sifted light brown sugar and slide baking dish under pre-heated broiler long enough to caramelize sugar. Leave oven door open and watch very closely so it does not burn! Serve at once.

HARRY'S MANGO BREAD

Pour 6 beaten egg yolks into blender and add 2 C oil, 3 C sugar, 2 t vanilla, and 4 C ripe mashed or chopped Hayden mangoes. Mix at medium speed to blend.

Transfer to mixing bowl, add 4 C flour sifted with 4 t baking soda, 1 t salt, and 4 t cinnamon. Add 1/2 C macadamia or walnuts, chopped, and 1 C grated coconut. Mix at medium speed until thoroughly mixed.

Turn into 5 greased and floured loaf pans and bake at 350 for 1 hr or until knife blade comes out clean. Cool in pans, turn out, and enjoy.

This freezes very well, too, hence the large recipe.

GRACE WARREN'S FAMOUS MANGO BREAD

Cream 1/2 C shortening with 3/4 C sugar and add 2 large beaten eggs.

Sift 3 C flour with 1 t baking soda, 1/4 t salt, and add alternately with 1 C diced ripe, juicy mangoes sprinkled with 1 T lemon juice. Fold in 1/2 C chopped walnuts or pecans. Turn into well greased loaf pan and bake 1 hr in 375 oven.

MANGO CHICKEN

Coat 4 lbs chicken thighs with a mixture of flour, seasonings, and curry to taste. Fry in sesame oil to brown until golden. Roll in paper towels to remove grease, and put pieces in casserole as they are cooked.

To the frying pan add 1 12-oz can orange juice, the juice of 1 lime, 1/2 of a 7-oz jar of preserved ginger, chopped in small pieces, S&P, and brown sugar to taste.

Scrape the bottom of pan and simmer gently for 10 mins, keep stirring, and add 2 C or more of rather large slices of ripe but firm mangoes. Pour over chicken and bake slowly for an hour in 325 oven. Serve with fluffy, white rice.

MULBERRIES

In days of yore, most every kamaaina home had a mulberry tree growing in the yard, and the kids used to take great delight in "casing the trees" for the silk worm cocoons feeding on the leaves, and then munching the sweet, seedless, ripe fruit.

The inch long fruit ripens from a green to shades of pink and red until, when dead ripe, a purplish-bluish-black. These delicate fruits were a great favorite of adults, if they got there before the birds, and delicious served with sugar and cream, made into fabulous pies, tasty juices and sherbets.

MULBERRY PIE

Prepare your favorite pie crust recipe or use frozen pie shells.

Combine 1 C sugar, 4 T flour and 1/4 t salt and sprinkle about a quarter of the mixture over the pie shell. Add 3 C washed berries and sprinkle the remaining mixture over them. Cover all with the top crust, bake in 450 oven for 10 mins, and reduce heat to 350. Bake 30 mins more or until nicely brown. Try it with vanilla ice cream over the top!!

NOTES

Plumeria Lei in Calabash   *Courtesy of Mrs. Miriam Rogers*

MAY

◆

May is here, tra, la, la, la, la, la!

Hawaii is bursting with spring flowers...scented gardenias and stephanotis, sturdy agapanthus lilies and day lilies, colorful plumeria trees, and varied-colored shower trees.

Watch out for Spring Fever!

Ever since 1928 when Don Blanding and Grace Tower Warren originated the idea, Hawaii has celebrated Lei Day on May 1st. It's a day when everyone wears a lei and a smile, Maypole dances are replaced by Lei Day Queens and their courts, and Lei Day Contests bring out the keenest of competition for a variety of leis and prizes.

The second Sunday in May is Mother's Day. Make it special starting with breakfast.

The traditional Memorial Day falls on the 30th, but is celebrated over the nearest long weekend.

Papayas are at their height!

As the Lei Day Queen and her courts are made up of beautiful people of various racial mixtures, so are the cuisines of the Islands.

Hawaii's universally popular and favorite foods are a mixture of dishes originating from all the ethnic groups who have migrated to these Islands from around the world and earned Hawaii the title, "Melting Pot of the Pacific."

ISLAND FAVORITES

POKE (Hawaiian Raw Fish)

Cut 1 lb red fish in cubes. Combine 1/2 C chopped limu, 1 T Hawaiian salt or to taste, 1/2 t chopped kukui nut, 4 chopped green onions, and mix into fish with your fingers to coat well. If you like it spicy hot, add chopped de-seeded Hawaiian chili peppers. Keep refrigerated until serving.

SASHIMI (Japanese Raw Fish)

Ahi is good for this dish, but any firm white fish is acceptable. The fish must be very fresh, and is easier to slice if it's really chilled. Remove skin, bones, and any dark portions of the fish.

Use a very sharp knife to cut the fillets in very thin slices. Carefully slide knife under sliced fish and place on shredded cabbage or grated turnips and serve with a soy and mustard sauce.

Sauce: make a thick paste mixing 1/2 t dry mustard with 1/2 to 1 t water, then add 1 to 3 T soy slowly to blend well. Adjust to preference.

TAHITIAN RAW FISH

Cut fish into small cubes or slices. Cover with lime juice completely and let stand for several hours in refrigerator. Pour off juice and cover with coconut milk and S&P to taste. Some like to add sliced sweet onions. Keep refrigerated until serving.

NEW ENGLAND FISH CHOWDER

Cook fish bones and the head of fresh fish in salted water to cover. When done, remove meat and save stock. In a large frying pan or another pot, fry small slices of bacon until done, add chopped onions, and cook until golden brown. Add cubed potatoes and stock to cover. Simmer until potatoes are done. Add cooked fish which has been carefully de-boned, milk or half-and-half, and season with S&P, dill, rosemary, and Worcestershire Sauce to taste.

If you like a thicker chowder, grate in the potatoes and cook with onions and bacon until it thickens the stock. Then gradually pour in half-and-half and the fish and seasonings.

Always serve with hard tack.

PORTUGUESE BEAN SOUP

In a large pot, combine 1 lb Portuguese sausage, sliced, 1 large carrot, diced, 2 potatoes, diced, 2 small onions, chopped, 1 qt water, 2 8-oz cans tomato sauce, 1 clove garlic, minced, 1 bay leaf, and 1 T salt. Bring to a boil, lower heat, and simmer 20 mins, covered.

Add 2 15-oz cans kidney beans, 1 large head cabbage, chopped, and 1 C cooked macaroni. Simmer for 20 mins more. Re-check seasoning.

FRIED RICE

Heat heavy skillet and fry 6 sliced pieces of bacon until brown. Remove bacon but leave drippings in pan and saute 1 stalk slivered celery, 4 string beans cut French style, 1 small onion, chopped, 6 soaked and sliced dry mushrooms, 1/2 C thinly sliced carrot sticks, and cook while stirring.

Add 3 C cold rice and keep stirring to break down chunks. When all is blended, break in 2 eggs, slightly beaten, and distribute well. Add 2 T soy or more, 1/2 t sugar, and S&P to taste. Keep stirring, add 4 stalks chopped green onions, and steam 10 mins.

Instead of bacon, fry up 1 C diced ham in oil.

CHICKEN AND LONG RICE

Soak 1 bundle long rice in water to soften; drain.

Pour 2 slightly beaten eggs into large heated, buttered pan and fry like pancake. Remove and cut into strips.

Fry 2 cloves minced garlic and 1 small thumb of ginger, slivered, in 2 T oil until brown. Remove and add 2-1/2 - 3 lbs chicken cut into bite-size pieces and fry until lightly browned. Add 4 C water and cook until the chicken is tender.

Add long rice, 1 T ea salt and soy, or to taste, simmer 15 mins more, and re-check flavoring. Add 1 C or more of chopped green onions. Turn into serving bowl and top with eggs.

CHINESE SPARERIBS
WITH SWEET AND SOUR SAUCE

In heavy pot cook 2 lbs spare ribs with 1-1/2 C water for about 40 mins or until tender. Lift from the broth and save broth to use in sauce.

Heat 2 T oil and fry spareribs only to brown. In same pan saute 1 sliced onion, 1 carrot thinly sliced, and 1 small piece ginger, shredded.

Mix together for Sweet and Sour Sauce: 1/2 C sugar, 1/4 C soy, 3/4 C vinegar, and 1 T cornstarch. Add to the vegetables and spareribs in pan, bring to a boil, then add the broth. Simmer for 1/2 hr longer.

NAMASU (Japanese Cucumber Salad)

Peel and slice 4 medium size cucumbers very thin, sprinkle with 1-1/2 T salt, let stand 20 mins, and drain. Press out excess water, but don't rinse.

Measure 1/2 C sugar and 1/2 t salt into a bowl, add 1/2 C either white or Japanese vinegar and 1 t chopped ginger, and mix until sugar is dissolved. Add 1 can minced clams, with juice, and cucumbers. Toss well and chill.

PORK CHOP SUEY

Cut 1 lb lean pork into strips and soak in 2 T soy, and 1 T bourbon, and a few drops of ginger juice.

Cut the following vegetables into strips and pan fry until crispy: 1 large carrot, 1/2 lb string beans, 2 round onions, 1 C green onion, 4 stalks celery, 1/2 lb broccoli, 1 small can mushrooms or 8 dried and soaked mushrooms, 2 C bamboo shoots, sliced, and 1/2 lb chop suey potato.

Heat saucepan, add 2 T oil and 1 clove crushed garlic. Add pork and cook for a few minutes. Add 1/2 C chopped ham and cook until pork is well done. Then add blanched vegetables, 2 C soup stock, and bring to simmer.

Thicken with 2 T cornstarch mixed with 1 T sugar and 1/4 C soy, bring to boil, mix well, turn to low, cover, and keep warm to serve.

TERIYAKI SAUCE

Combine 3/4 C soy, 5 T sugar, 1 large piece ginger, crushed, 1 clove garlic, crushed, and mix well. Soak meat according to taste.

THE ALL TIME FAVORITES

A plate of steaming hot rice, fried rings of Portuguese sausage, and scrambled eggs...with chili pepper water and catsup.

Fried Spam, brown and crispy, served with sunny-side-up eggs and hash brown potatoes.

Saloon pilots slathered with Borden's sweetened condensed milk.

MOTHER'S DAY

This is the day that conjures up visions of a beaming mother sitting up in bed greeting her children with a "Oh, how wonderful!" as they present her with a tray for her breakfast in bed. It may not be anything spectacular, but a lot of love went into the preparation.

Maybe the following may be of some help later.

EGGS

When cooking eggs, especially scrambled, don't rush them. They tend to get tough. Cook eggs slowly, and preferably at room temperature, not cold.

If you have a household of staggered risers, use a double boiler to scramble eggs and they'll remain hot, moist and creamy until served.

Don't add too much milk, cream or water to scrambled eggs, otherwise they'll be watery. Beat the eggs until yolks and whites are mixed and pour into well buttered pan over low heat. Keep stirring until the mixture is the consistency of soft custard: set, but more on the soft, moist side.

Experiment with various additions to plain scrambled eggs.

Add your favorite garden herbs, sauteed onions and fresh sliced mushrooms, slivers of sharp cheddar cheese, minced ham and finely chopped green onion or peppers, tuna and finely chopped green onions, or cottage cheese and chives.

CURRIED SCRAMBLED EGGS WITH LOBSTER

Heat 3/4 C cooked lobster or crab pieces in 3 T butter. Stir almost constantly but don't let it boil, add dash of paprika, a T or less of curry, and S&P to taste.

Beat 7 eggs as for an omelet with 1/3 C heavy cream and pour all at once over mixture. Stir gently over a low heat until eggs just begin to set. Serve over buttered toast and garnish with crisp watercress and wedges of tomato.

POACHED EGGS IN CREAM

In a frying pan add 1 C ea cream and milk, season, and heat but don't boil. When hot, drop in 6 eggs one at a time, cover, and cook slowly about 5 mins, then sprinkle with 1 C grated cheese and paprika. When eggs are set, place on buttered toast and pour cream over all.

Try poaching eggs in consomme or cream of tomato soup for a change.

BAKED EGGS

For each serving mix 1 T ea chopped fresh parsley and green onions and 2 T minced ham in individual ramekins. Break 2 eggs over. Drizzle 1 T heavy cream over eggs and season to taste with S&P.

Place ramekins in pan with hot water coming to within 1 in up the dish. Bake 15 mins or longer, depending on how you like your eggs. Serve with de-crusted and buttered thin slices of toast.

STEPHEN REED'S HUEVOS RANCHEROS

Fry 4 tortillas in 3 T oil, remove, and keep hot. To the oil add 1 T minced onion and 1 small clove garlic, minced, and saute 2 mins. Add 1 T minced parsley, 1 C tomato sauce, 1/2 t ea coriander, basil, and marjoram. Blend and simmer for 3 mins.

Place 2 poached or fried eggs on each tortillas, cover with sauce, and top with slices of avocado and pieces of pimento. Serves 4.

FRENCH TOAST

Trim crusts from 6 slices of white bread. Combine 4 beaten eggs, 2 t sugar, 1/2 t salt, pinch of baking powder, 3/4 t vanilla, 1/4 t nutmeg or cinnamon, and 1/2 C ea milk and half-and-half. Stir well with fork. Carefully dip slices of bread in mixture to absorb liquid and fry quickly in hot greased pan until golden brown on both sides. Serve with syrup, honey, jelly, or powdered sugar.

CHEESY FRENCH TOAST

Combine 1 C grated sharp cheese, 2 eggs, and 1/2 C cream and whip to blend. Dip 8 slices of white bread into mixture until well coated. Fry in hot skillet with 3 T each of butter and oil until golden brown on both sides, and serve with marmalade.

DIFFERENT PANCAKES

Combine 4 slices raisin bread, 4 eggs, 1/4 C water, 7 t sugar, and 1/2 t vanilla in blender and whir until batter is smooth. Heat skillet, add oil, and when hot drop batter by tablespoonfuls to cook until bubbles appear. Turn pancakes to brown other side. Serve with strawberry or other preserves.

COTTAGE CHEESE PANCAKES

In blender combine 3 eggs, well beaten, 2 T salad oil or melted butter, 1/4 C flour, 1 C sieved small-curd cottage cheese, and 1/2 t salt and mix well. Drop by spoonfuls on hot griddle. Roll up pancakes with hot applesauce for filling and serve with powdered sugar and cinnamon.

DICK HEDLUND'S LAZY GUY PANCAKES

Fry 3/4 or 1 lb chopped bacon in pan to medium done, pour off excess grease, and set aside.

Mix your favorite hot cake or waffle batter (2 C Bisquick, 1 C milk, 2 eggs) and beat 'em up. Pour mixture over bacon in pan and bake in 375 oven until it rises and is crispy brown on top. Cut it like cake, load with butter and syrup, and no need to wait in between cooking.

WAFFLES

Sift 2 C flour, 4 t baking powder, 1/4 t salt, and 2 T sugar.

Beat 2 egg yolks and add 1-1/2 C milk. Stir into dry ingredients and beat until batter is smooth. Add 6 T melted butter and fold in 2 stiffly beaten whites. Preheat iron and pour in batter to bake 3-4 mins. Makes 6.

Add grated rind of 1 orange and 2 t juice to batter.

Add 1 t cinnamon for more flavor.

RED FLANNEL HASH

In small skillet, saute 3/4 C chopped onion in 2 T melted butter until soft. Add 3 C cooked chopped potatoes, 1-1/2 C diced beets, 2 C canned or cooked corn beef, chopped, and 1-1/2 C dairy sour cream. Season with S&P to taste. In skillet, fry mixture slowly in 3 T butter till bottom is crusty. Invert platter over skillet and turn out so crusty side is up.

Poach eggs separately and place on top. Serves 6.

BRUNCH RED FLANNEL HASH AND EGGS

Combine 1/4 C chopped green or white onion, 1-1/2 C chopped corn beef, 1 10-oz can beets, drained and chopped, 2-1/2 C cooked diced potatoes, 1/3 C beef broth, and mix all together well. Shape into 6 patties and fry in oleo till brown on each side. Keep warm.

Fry 6 eggs in 2 T oleo, sunny side up. Toast 12 slices of bread, spread with butter and garlic salt.

Place hot patties on warm plate, top with eggs, and serve with toast cut diagonally.

RICH BISCUITS

Rub 6 T butter into 2 C flour, add 6 T sugar, 1/2 t baking powder, and if you like, 1 t either caraway or poppy seeds. Beat 1 egg and fold into flour mixture to blend.

Roll into little balls with hands, flatten on cookie sheet, and bake in 350 oven 10 mins.

This is like shortbread but less rich.

SCRUMPTIOUS CORN BREAD

Sift together 1/2 C flour, 1 t salt, 1-1/4 t baking soda, and add 2 C cornmeal, 1 C wheat germ, and 1/2 C sesame seeds.

Mix together 1/4 C honey, 1 C ea buttermilk and cottage cheese, 1/4 C oil, and 3 large eggs. Add liquid ingredients all at once to the dry ingredients, and stir until the dry ingredients are thoroughly moistened.

Turn batter into a buttered 9x13 in pan. Bake in 375 oven for 45 mins or until lightly browned and inserted wooden toothpick comes out clean.

HALEKULANI'S FAMOUS POPOVERS

Beat in a bowl 2 eggs until light. Add 1 C milk, 1 T melted butter or margarine, 1 C flour, and 1/4 t salt. Beat until evenly blended. Batter should be like heavy cream. Pour into heavily greased muffin pan or glass or pottery cups. Fill mixture to the top.

Bake 20 mins at 450, reduce oven heat to 350, and bake about 30 to 40 mins. Do not remove immediately from the oven. Move pans to the front of the oven and allow to stand with oven door open to reduce heat gradually. Makes 4 large popovers.

MYRNA OSHIMA'S
CINNAMON SOUR CREAM COFFEE CAKE

Batter: cream 1 C butter with 1-1/4 C sugar until fluffy, add 2 eggs, and beat well. Add 1 C dairy sour cream to blend.

Sift 2 C flour with 1/4 t ea baking soda and baking powder, add to cream mixture, and blend in 1 t vanilla.

Mix together 3/4 C chopped macadamia nuts or walnuts, 1 t cinnamon, and 2 T sugar. Divide 1/2 of batter into 2 8x4x2 in loaf pans, then sprinkle cinnamon-nut mix over top. Divide second 1/2 of batter, spoon it over filling, and top with the cinnamon mixture. Bake in 350 oven for 40 to 50 mins.

ICE CREAM MUFFINS

In a bowl mix together 1-1/4 C flour, 1/4 C packed brown sugar, 2-1/2 t baking powder, 1/2 t salt, and 1/4 t ground cinnamon. Combine 1 beaten egg with 1 C macadamia nut ice cream or butter brickle, softened, and 1/3 C cooking oil.

Stir liquid into dry ingredients just until moistened. Fill greased muffin pans 2/3 full. Bake in 375 oven for 18-20 mins. Makes 10-12 muffins.

NUTTY BANANA MUFFINS

Preheat oven to 425.

Combine 2 C pancake mix, 1/4 C sugar, 1/2 t cinnamon, and 1/2 C nuts in a bowl. Add 1 beaten egg, 3/4 C milk, and 1/2 C mashed bananas. Stir and add 3 T oil or 1/2 stick melted butter. Stir only until combined. You may add 1/2 C chopped nuts.

Fill greased muffin cups 3/4 full and bake for 15-20 mins.

NORMA JOINER'S ONO MUFFINS

Mix together 2 C Bisquick, 1 bottle blue label Avoset, and 1 T sugar. Bake in greased muffin pan in 350 oven for 20 mins.

Really light and full of calories!!!

BREAKFAST TREAT

Whip softened butter with guava jam to taste. Place in pretty bowl and leave on table to spread over toasted Portuguese sweet bread.

MILK TOAST

Place a slice of de-crusted and buttered toast in a deep dish. Add a speck of salt to 1 C of hot milk and pour over the toast. Serve at once.

Especially good when you are feeling under the weather.

MUESLI

This is a breakfast food, full of natural grains and roughage.

In a large bowl combine: 1 C rolled oats, 1/2 C each unprocessed bran, processed crunchy bran, wheat germ, sultanas, chopped raisins, and dried coconut, 2 T ea sesame, sunflower, or any other favorite seeds, and finely chopped dried fruits...apples, prunes, apricots, dates, etc. Mix thoroughly and store in tightly capped container.

Enjoy with cream, yogurt or milk. Or sprinkle on top of halved papaya and top with yogurt. If you don't add freshly chopped candied or dried fruit in the mixture, you may add freshly chopped canned or dried fruit at each serving.

FRUIT

PAPAYA

May and June are the peak months for papaya, the versatile fruit. It can be cooked green or ripe, baked, stewed or raw, served as a fruit for breakfast, salad at lunch, and a vegetable or a dessert at dinner. Any other time it can be used in jams, chutney, juice, or candied, and its flowers can be strung into leis. The leaves can be used to wrap the tougher pieces of meat to tenderize them.

BAKED PAPAYA

Cut papaya in half, remove seeds, and peel off outer skin. Cut slices into casserole, drizzle lemon juice over them, sprinkle nutmeg over all, and dot with butter. Bake in 350 oven for at least 30 mins.

PAPAYA MARMALADE

Combine 10 C firm, ripe papaya, sliced, 1 C fresh shredded pineapple, 1/2 C orange juice, grated rind of 1 orange and 2 lemons, 3 T grated ginger, and 1/2 C lemon juice. Stir and boil for 30 mins.

Measure cooked fruit, add an equal measure of sugar, and cook for 30 mins, stirring frequently to prevent burning. Pour into sterilized jars, seal with paraffin, label, and store in cool place.

PAPAYA STUFFING SQUARES

Butter 7 slices of white bread, break into pieces, and place in greased 9x9x2 in baking dish. Beat 4 eggs with 1/2 C sugar, add puree of 2 papayas mixed with juice and rind of one lemon, and pour over bread. Bake 40 mins in 350 oven, cut into squares, and serve hot with yogurt or cream. Serves 4.

PAPAYA CAKE

Cream 1/2 C shortening with 1-1/2 C sugar, add 2 eggs one at a time, beating well after each addition. Add 2 C diced papaya and beat well. Sift 3 C flour with 2 t soda, 1 t ea cinnamon and salt, 1/2 t ea nutmeg and ginger, and add to mixture with 2 T water and juice of 1 lemon or 1 t.

Fold in 1 C floured raisins, pour into oiled 12x9x2 in pan, and bake at 325 for 45 to 50 mins.

PAPAYA COOKIES

Cream 1/2 C butter with 1 C sugar, add 1 egg slightly beaten. Add 1 t baking soda to 1/2 C pureed papaya, stir to mix, and add to sugar mixture with 1 t almond extract.

Combine 2 C flour with 1 t ea baking powder and mace, 1/2 t salt, add to bowl, and mix thoroughly. Chill for 1 hr and drop by teaspoonfuls onto greased cookie sheet. Bake 12 to 15 mins in 375 oven or until light brown. Remove from cookie sheet, cool on cooking rack, and store when cool.

BAKED FRESH PAPAYA WITH CURRY

Cut papayas in half and de-seed. Fill cavity with chicken curry and sprinkle flaked, unsweetened coconut over the top. Bake halves in 350 oven 10-15 mins and garnish with lime slice or chutney.

PAPAYA CHUTNEY

Boil 2-1/4 C vinegar and 3-1/2 C raw sugar for a few minutes. Add 2 T ginger root, chopped fine, 3 de-seeded chili peppers, chopped fine, and 1 clove minced garlic and cook a little longer. Add 3-1/4 qts cubed or sliced papaya (firm but not too ripe), 3 C seedless raisins, and 1-1/4 t salt. Cook until mixture thickens to desired consistency, stirring so as not to burn. Pour into hot sterile glasses and seal. Yields 6 pts.

PAPAYA GINGER MARMALADE

Cook 2 lemons, thinly sliced and cut in halves, in 2 C of water for 30 mins or until transparent. Make a syrup of 1 t finely chopped ginger and 4 C ea water and sugar by boiling until it threads. Pour over 8 C sliced, firm, ripe papaya and lemons and boil slowly about 30 mins or until it thickens. Pour into hot sterile glasses and seal with paraffin. 2 qts.

PAPAYA PICKLE

Make a syrup of 4 C sugar and 2 C vinegar by cooking for 6-8 mins. Add 12 cloves, 16 peppercorns, and 4 bay leaves.

Cook 8 C half-ripe papaya slices in 2 C water for 5 mins, drain, and add fruit to the syrup. Cook mixture about 15 mins, pour into sterilized jars, and seal immediately. 2 qts.

NOTES

Yellow Ginger   *Courtesy of Mrs. Thurmond Clarke*

JUNE

It's June! School's Out!!
Time for graduation, wedding bells,
and the simple living that goes
with summertime.

June 11th is the birthday of King Kamehameha I, the Napoleon of the Pacific who united all the islands and created a dynasty that lasted for 75 years. Hawaii salutes our hero with special activities and parades on all the islands.

The third Sunday of the month is Father's Day. Crown him with love and attention!

This is the season for guavas, lychees, mountain apples, strawberry guavas, and passion fruit.

Familiarize yourself with our local produce and include them in your menus.

KAMEHAMEHA AND NATIVE FOODS

During the reign of Kamehameha I, he observed the strict rules of the ancient Hawaiian religion. Sacred heiaus were maintained, and the many kapu customs observed.

The disciplinary rules dictated what you ate, how you fished, when you fought, and relationships with your fellow man. Religious tabus not only restricted women from eating with men, but from eating certain varieties of bananas, coconuts, pork, and certain seafoods.

Having brought peace to the Islands, Kamehameha encouraged the people to persevere in raising food on land long ravaged by civil wars. A farmer and fisherman at heart, Kamehameha led the way by tilling the land himself. Eventually breadfruit, coconut, sweet potatoes, yams, bananas, water melons, pumpkins, cabbages, and other food plants flourished and are still enjoyed today.

Living along the seashore and streams, Hawaiians were expert fishermen, and fish, raw or cooked, was an important part of their diet. A variety of crabs, lobster, opihi, pipii, wana (sea urchin), and squid all added a change of flavor to the diet.

Poi was the staff of life; wet and dry-land taro, both tops and bottoms, sweet potatoes, coconuts, and bananas were their principal vegetables. Pork was their only meat until later when cattle were introduced by Vancouver, and limu, salt, and kukui nuts were their sole relishes.

The men were responsible for providing and preparing food for the family. They tended the taro patches, pounded poi, went fishing, and prepared the imu in which to cook large quantities of food to last for many days.

Briefly, here are some of the basic Hawaiian dishes that have survived to the present day.

POI Taro root that has been cooked, peeled, pounded and kneaded with water to a smooth paste-like consistency that can be lifted gracefully from the bowl to the mouth with 1 or 2 fingers.

KALUA PUA'A A suckling pig; cleaned, rubbed with Hawaiian salt inside and out, its opu cavity filled with hot stones and placed in a pit lined with hot stones, ti and banana leaves. Then all is covered with more leaves, damp gunny sacks, and dirt and left to steam for several hours. (Don't try this one alone!)

LAULAU A puolo of taro leaves, chunks of fresh Island belly pork (and/or beef and chicken), and butterfish or salt salmon securely wrapped and tied with ti leaves. This is either added to the imu or steamed over simmering water for at least 4 hours.

If using only pork, use 1/2 lb pork and 15 taro leaves and sprinkle with Hawaiian salt. Instead of pork use chicken thighs.

I'A LAWALU A scaled and cleaned whole fresh fish, salted inside and out, securely wrapped in ti leaves, and steamed in the imu or in the oven.

MOA LUAU Whole stewing chicken, cooked, and chopped in serving pieces, combined with cooked taro leaves and coconut cream. (Modern version: 2 lbs thighs, cooked, de-boned and skinned, 2 packages frozen spinach, and 1 can thawed coconut cream with salt to taste.)

KAMANO LOMI Salt salmon that has been soaked for at least 3 hours in several changes of water, shredded by hand, and lomi-ed with peeled and seeded fresh tomatoes. Add chopped green onions, mix thoroughly, and serve sprinkled with chipped ice. (1 lb salmon and 6 large tomatoes. Serve chopped green onions separately.)

HE'E AND LUAU Tenderized squid cut up and cooked with luau leaves and coconut cream.

DRIED HE'E AND I'A Squid and fish dried in the sun.

KULOLO A pudding made with grated raw taro mixed with coconut milk and raw sugar to taste, and steamed in the imu or over boiling water for several hours until thoroughly cooked. Served cold, cut into cubes.

HAUPIA A sweet pudding made of heated coconut cream thickened with cornstarch and sweetened to taste. Cool and cut into squares to serve cold.

INAMONA Dry kukui nuts roasted, shelled, and the kernels pounded together with coarse Hawaiian salt to form a smooth, oily paste.

SWEET POTATOES AND BANANAS Baked in the imu or boiled.

THE POI SUPPER

A beautifully appointed poi supper is one of the most gracious and hospitable ways of entertaining in the Islands. It need not be an elaborate meal including a great variety of foods, however; basically, the menu should include either kalua pig or individual laulaus, chicken luau, lomi salmon, lawalu fish, poi, condiments of red salt, green onions, kukui nut, limu, and dried fish, baked bananas or sweet potatoes, and haupia.

If you wish to include baked fish in your menu, instead of baking the whole fish, cut it into serving pieces, sprinkle with Hawaiian salt, wrap separately in a ti leaf, and then place bundles in oven to bake or steam.

Fortunately, in most areas there is a reliable family fish market that dispenses delicious Hawaiian food which alleviates almost all the cooking so that you can concentrate on your table, which is so important in setting the mood of the meal. If possible, a long table for 8 or 12 is ideal.

Cover the table with an old cloth, then lay clean, ribbed, green ti leaves down in a herring bone pattern with ti leaves down the middle to hide the leaf ends from both sides. Cover this with fresh, lacy ferns and use a watermelon sliced Van Dyke-style and/or crowned pineapples that have been cut out in serving pieces as centerpieces, interspersed with colorful fresh fruit (ripe papayas, yellow bananas, grapes, etc.).

Or else strew flowers or lay leis down the middle and around low candles. Use your imagination, but keep the arrangements low and leave lots of room for the individual dishes needed in front of each guest.

Set each place with a wine glass, finger bowl filled with warm water and a slice of lemon or sweet geranium leaf, and a folded dinner napkin. Remember - fingers came before forks and spoons, and silverware is not mandatory! When the guests are seated, there should be a dish of condiments and a serving of poi and salmon lomi at each place. After the guests are seated, serve the hot laulaus, chicken, and fish. It is important that you serve the cold food cold and the hot food hot! Luau food is to be savored and enjoyed, so make it a leisurely meal.

Old-time kamaaina hostesses serve food in individual coconut and glass dishes which are kept exclusively for a poi supper. It does enhance the decor if you serve food in matching bowls and dishes. (Inexpensive glass or lacquer bowls are nice, too.)

The fruit and haupia is sufficient for dessert, but a fresh coconut cake is even better!

Since Hawaiian food is rather filling, keep the pupus simple. Macadamia nuts, taro chips, arare, Japanese crackers, or raw vegetables with a dip are good choices.

HAWAIIAN KAUKAU AWAY FROM THE ISLANDS

Those of you on the mainland, too, can have a poi supper with a bit of ingenuity, substitutions, exotic Hawaiian drinks, a full-out Polynesian tapa paper table cloth, flowers, and paper leis!

OVEN KALUA PIG

Score the fat of a 5 lb pork butt into 1 in squares and rub with Hawaiian or plain salt. Sprinkle Bar-B-Q Smoke Liquid over all sides of the meat and into the fat. Wrap securely in tin foil and bake in 325 oven for at least 4 hrs. Undo the foil and brown the fat to a crisp. Shred the meat off the bones as they do for kalua pig.

Throw in a pan of baking bananas or sweet potatoes the last 1-1/2 hr.

CHICKEN LUAU

In a casserole place 2 packages thawed, chopped spinach, 2 lbs chicken thighs, sprinkle with onion chips and 1 t sugar, then pour 1 can thawed coconut milk over. Bake in 375 oven until chicken is done, about an hr. Thicken with a paste of cornstarch and water. Check seasoning and add salt.

Salmon Lomi isn't any problem if you can find salt salmon in the market.

Skin, cut up in chunks, and soak in several changes of water until not too salty. Skin tomatoes, crush with fingers, and add shredded salmon. Serve icy cold. (1 lb salmon to 9-12 tomatoes.) Serve chopped green onions separately.

If you can't find salt salmon, a good brand of canned red sockeye salmon will suffice.

Use any fish, but wrap in foil instead of leaves.

For a condiment dish, include coarse salt, green onions, a few boiled shrimp, salt mackerel, and as a substitute for kukui nut chop up walnuts and roast them with salt in slow oven for half an hour.

Pass the pineapple or pick up packages of Haupia Pudding for dessert when you're in Hawaii! Aloha Kau-Kau!

ISLAND PRODUCE

TARO

Taro is one of the oldest known vegetables in the Islands, having been brought by the exploring Polynesians in their double-hulled canoes from the South Pacific. It was the staff of life to the natives.

Once mastered, cooking taro can be just as simple as boiling Irish potatoes. Wash corms to remove any dirt and cook thoroughly in 3 changes of water until tender...like potatoes. If not thoroughly cooked, crystals of calcium oxalate react on the tongue, mouth, and throat like prickly needles and can be pretty unpleasant.

When still hot, peel taro and mash over low heat with as little water as possible, or cut up and use as you wish...in salads, stews, chips, or fried.

To prepare the taro leaves (luau), wash bunches, snip off tough part of stalk, and peel off the thickest of the veins from the stalk and on into the leaves. Snip off both ends of folded leaves, too. Put in large pot with just enough water to simmer. The leaves will soon wilt down considerably. Change the water at least three times and boil until tender...about an hour...over low heat. Serve as spinach with S&P and butter, use in lau laus, or with chicken and coconut cream.

Ha-ha is the stem of the taro leaf. Peel off tough outside, chop, and cook until tender in changes of water. Serve with butter and S&P as a vegetable.

Or fry pieces of sliced pork in oil with garlic and onion, stir fry until gray, and add water. Bring to a boil, add chopped ha-ha, and cook until soft. Add soy to taste.

TARO CAKES

Boil peeled taro until very tender, almost mushy, and mash until smooth while still hot. Use as little water as possible.

To one cup mashed taro add 1 t each baking powder and salt and 1 T sugar. Wet your hands and form the mixture into small cakes. Place them on buttered cookie sheet, press in a pat of butter on top of each, and bake in 350 oven for about 25 mins or until brown and crispy.

TARO CAKE PUPU

Make taro cakes as above, but add Hawaiian red salt to taste, bits of cooked Portuguese sausage, and chopped green onions, green and all. Bake in 350 oven until brown and crispy.

WASHINGTON PLACE TARO CAKE (During Governor Lawrence M. Judd's time.)

Combine 1 C hot boiled mashed taro with 1 t baking powder, 1 T sugar, and 1/4 t salt. Put in small muffin pans, pat level, and bake in hot oven for 30 mins. If mixed when hot, add no water.

POI MUFFINS

Combine 1 C poi, 2/3 C buttermilk, 2 eggs, and 1/2 C oil. Combine 2 C flour, 3 t baking powder, 1/4 t baking soda, 3 T sugar, and 1/2 t salt. Mix wet and dry ingredients together until moistened. Turn into greased muffin pan and bake at 350 for 30 mins. Serve warm and pass the butter.

TARO CHIPS

Boil taro, peel, and chill thoroughly. Slice as thin as possible and fry in deep fat like potato chips. Spread on absorbent paper and sprinkle with salt while hot.

SATORU OKIHARA'S PRIZE WINNING TARO BREAD

Dissolve 1 package yeast in 1/2 C lukewarm water, add 1 T sugar, and let rise.

In electric mixer bowl beat: 1 egg, 1/2 C ea oil and sugar, 1-1/2 t salt, and 1 C steamed grated taro. Add yeast mixture and 2 C lukewarm water. From 7 C of flour, add enough till dough is stiff enough to put on floured board. Knead, keep on adding flour so dough will not stick on hand...about 8-10 mins.

Let rise in greased bowl till double in bulk (about 2-1/2 hrs). Punch down and shape into loaves and place into greased bread pans. Let rise till double in bulk, and bake loaves about 40 mins in 350 oven.

TARO CORNED BEEF HASH PUPU

Mix together: 3 C cooked and mashed taro, 1 finely chopped medium round or 6 green onions, 2 beaten eggs, 1 C corned beef chopped up, and S&P to taste. Pat to small ball size and pan fry until brown. Bigger size can be made into regular corned beef hash patties.

TARO BISCUIT

Combine and blend 1 C mashed cooked taro with 1/4 C soft shortening, add 1-1/2 C flour, 3 t baking powder, 2 t sugar, and 1/2 t salt and blend. Add 1 beaten egg and 1/4 C milk.

Knead on lightly floured board, pat into 1/2 in thickness, cut with biscuit cutter, and bake in 425 oven for 15 mins. Serve hot with lots of butter to enjoy.

GINGER

The piquant-flavored ginger root appears as an exotic ingredient in a variety of Island recipes. But these are not to be confused with the knobby roots of the inedible, tropical flowering varieties! The powdered ginger seasoning will never take the place of the fresh ginger root.

Ginger stored in plastic bags in the refrigerator should stay fresh for several weeks. Ginger may be chopped, minced, slivered, grated, cut in chunks, or squeezed through a garlic press for juice.

Many old-timers don't bother to scrape or peel off the dry outer skin, but simply scrub the root clean and use it.

Ginger is an essential ingredient in curries, chutney, namasu, and especially in a variety of marinades for meat, fowl, or fish.

Slice ginger against the grain.

Chop up preserved ginger and add this and some juice to softened vanilla ice cream for a special dessert treat.

ORANGE GINGER CHICKEN

In a large bowl combine 2/3 C orange juice, 1/4 C dry sherry, 1 T ea oil and grated fresh ginger, 1 clove minced garlic, 1 t salt, and 1/2 t basil.

Add 3 lbs chicken cut in frying pieces and toss to coat. Cover and refrigerate 6-8 hrs, turning occasionally.

Thoroughly drain chicken, reserving liquid. Place pieces in large shallow baking pan and bake in 400 oven for 25 mins. Drain off fat, pour reserved liquid over chicken, and continue to bake, basting occasionally, about 25 mins until chicken is browned and cooked. Transfer to serving dish and garnish with orange slices and parsley. Serve with pan juices. Serves 4 to 6.

SWEET POTATO

The original settlers of Hawaii brought the sweet potato with them and soon knew how well it went with pork and coconut, but we have since learned that sweet potatoes also blend well with oranges, lemons, apples, a touch of brown sugar, and marshmallows.

The sweet potato is not a tuber, but an elongated root. Both leaf top or shoots and the root are edible.

SWEET POTATO BISCUITS

Combine 3/4 C mashed sweet potatoes, 1 T brown sugar, salt to taste, 1/4 C melted butter, 1/3 C milk, and 1/3 C bourbon. Mix well to blend, then gradually work in 1-1/4 C flour combined with 2-1/2 t baking powder and 1 t salt.

Pat dough 1/2 in thick on waxed paper, cut into small rounds, and bake at 450 about 15 mins or until biscuits are golden brown and crusty.

SWEET POTATO PUFFS

Combine 2 C sweet potatoes, cooked and mashed, 1 large mashed banana, 2 T melted oleo, 1 beaten egg, 1-1/4 t salt, and add just enough milk by tablespoonfuls to make potatoes fluffy. Drop batter in mounds 1-2 in apart on greased cookie sheet. Bake in 350 oven for about 12 mins until heated through and slightly brown. Makes 6.

SWEET POTATO AND APPLE CASSEROLE

Layer 2 large sweet potatoes, parboiled and sliced, 4-6 Pippin or Granny Smith apples, sliced, and 1/2 an onion, sliced, and dot with butter on each layer. Cover casserole with foil and bake for 30 mins at 350 or until done. Especially good with pork.

CHAYOTE

A light green-colored summer squash that grows on a vine that can take over your entire garden if not watched. Pick the chayote when they are small, as the larger ones tend to be tough. Peel and remove the center seeds before cooking. It's delicious simply sliced, steamed, and served with S&P and butter.

Marinate slices in a vinaigrette sauce.

Cooked squash may be used in souffles mixed with grated Parmesan cheese and chopped sage.

They can be substituted for cucumbers in making pickles.

CHINESE CABBAGE OR WON BOK

One of the versatile members of the leafy and stem vegetable family. A cross between Romaine lettuce and celery with a crispy, crunchy mid-rib between lovely white to dark green, crepe-like leaves.

Chopped with a French dressing, it makes a crunchy salad.

Steam the chopped leaves briefly and serve with either butter or sesame oil and soy. You might prefer the stalks cooked a little longer than the leaves, so steam them first, then add leaves.

Add chopped leaves to clear Chicken Soup.

WATERCRESS

A nutritious green vegetable that is not only good to nibble on cleaned and dried, but adds spice to any salad, soup, or chop suey dish.

For a delightful cold soup, combine in blender container 1 bunch chopped watercress with 1 can cream of mushroom soup, curry powder, Worcestershire sauce, and seasoning to taste. Add half-and-half for desired consistency. Serve chilled with chopped chives on top.

WATERCRESS PORK

Heat 3/4 T oil in skillet and brown 1 lb lean pork cut in thin strips with 1 T crushed ginger and 2 cloves crushed garlic until well done, then remove latter. Season with S&P. Make a smooth paste of 1 T cornstarch, 1/2 C sugar, 2 t soy, and 1/2 C stock or water, and stir paste into the cooked meat. When liquid comes to a boil, add 1 bunch washed and chopped watercress, stems first then leafy pieces. Stir-fry about 2 mins until tender, cover, and serve hot over rice.

For a tasty salad, combine chopped watercress with fresh cubed mangoes and a French dressing.

For sandwiches, combine softened Philadelphia cream cheese with chopped or minced watercress, dash of Worcestershire sauce, and S&P to taste. Blend well and spread between very thin pieces of buttered bread.

PEPEIAO

This pinky-brown, fleshy, ear-shaped edible fungus (after the Hawaiian word for ear) thrives on rotting branches, especially after a heavy rain. They can be purchased in cellophane packets in dry form under the name Kikurage or Chin Nyee.

Fresh pepeiaos are a delicacy, more flavorful, and better textured. Some gourmet cooks prefer pepeiao over mushrooms, especially in hekka or namasu, and add them to other vegetables, fish, and meat dishes.

If you use the dry variety, soak Kikurage in salty water for 30 mins, wash clean, cut off stem ends, and chop or add whole.

LONG BEAN AND WINGED-BEAN

These beans are easy to grow, resemble the green bean, have similar taste, and can be used in the same way, yet each bean is slightly different.

Long beans last longer in the refrigerator, while wing beans are more perishable. Use the beans in salads, soups, and meat and fish dishes, but don't overcook them...5 mins at the most. Otherwise, the delicate flavor and texture are destroyed.

WINGED BEANS

Brown 1 clove minced garlic in 2 T hot oil till golden, add 2 C winged beans cut in 1/2 in pieces, and stir-fry till slightly cooked but still crisp. Add 1/2 C dry roasted peanuts and continue frying for 1 min. Sprinkle with 1 t toasted sesame seeds. Serve with brown or white rice.

LONG BEANS AND PORK

Fry 1 clove minced garlic in 2 T oil till golden brown, add 1 C thinly sliced raw pork, and stir-fry by tossing meat until browned and cooked. Add 1/4 t black pepper and 2 C long beans sliced in 1/2 in pieces. Continue stir-frying by tossing until beans are tender but not soft. You may substitute cooked leftover meat. Serve with rice.

BEAN SPROUTS

These make a good addition to any salad. Blanche sprouts in boiling water for about a min, drain, and chill. Just before serving, add Japanese vinegar and sprinkling of sesame seeds.

Add sprouts at last minute to any stir-fry meat and vegetable dish.

CHINESE PEAS (Snow or Sugar Peas)

These can be steamed and served with butter or added to salads, raw or blanched, and chop suey dishes.

Snap off ends and string as much as possible, as they do tend to be very stringy.

JICAMA (Mexican Potato or Chinese Mountain Yams, Alias Chop Suey Yams)

These add crunch to many dishes, and a good substitute for water chestnuts.

Peel and cut into sticks to add to raw vegetable platters with dip.

GUAVAS

Guavas are not to be found in the markets, but still can be gathered from trees growing wild along the roadside or in the mountains. The normal season is summer, but can be found as late as November. Because of their high nutritive value, greater use should be made of guavas, especially for their high Vitamin C content. One ripe guava will supply more than the daily Vitamin C requirement of an adult!

The best way to preserve the fruit is by freezing. A basic guava pulp can be used when needed in puddings, cakes, ice cream, sherbets, jams, or candies. You may mix it with other fruit juices or dilute with water and use as a beverage.

If you find yourself with a bucket of guavas, here is what to do. Discard over-ripe guavas and use only firm, yellow, mature but slightly under ripe fruit, with some half ripe ones for pectin. Wash and slice or quarter them into a large pot. Fill with just enough water so you can barely see it beneath the fruit. Less water, faster cooking and lighter jelly.

Boil till soft and mushy, cool, and pour into jelly bags or several layers of cheesecloth to drip overnight. Don't press down on the bag or disturb it, just let it drip naturally for clear jelly.

Put remaining pulp left in bag in ricer to puree for jam or freeze it.

GUAVA JELLY

Bring 3 C fresh guava juice to boil in large pan. After it reaches a good rolling boil, add 3 C sugar and let it boil hard. Skim off scum and keep testing syrup until you can hold a spoonful of juice over the pot and it falls in sheets off the spoon.

Remove from heat, let it sit a bit, then pour into sterilized jars. Cool and add melted parawax to seal.

GUAVA JAM

Combine 4 C raw guava puree to 3 - 3-1/2 C sugar and bring to boil in large flat-bottom pan. Keep stirring frequently so it won't burn, but be careful of the spluttering puree.

After 30-40 mins it should have thickened enough to pour into sterilized jars and cover with parawax.

GUAVA MUFFINS

Sift together 2 C flour, 1 t ea salt and baking soda, and 2 t baking powder.

Combine 1/2 C guava puree, 1/4 C ea fresh milk and strong black coffee.

Cream 1/2 C shortening with 1 C granulated sugar and add 3 well-beaten eggs. Add the liquid alternately with the flour mixture until well blended.

Bake at 325 in well greased muffin tins for 30 mins or until tester comes out clean. 12 muffins.

GUAVA DRESSING

Combine following in blender container: 1 C ea mayonnaise and tomato catsup, 1/4 C vinegar, 1/2 C oil, 1 t dry mustard, 2 t lemon juice, 1/2 C guava jelly or jam, garlic salt to taste, and sugar if needed.

Blend well and chill.

GUAVA WHIP

Fold 1 C of guava puree into two beaten egg whites, sweeten to taste, chill, and serve in sherbet glasses, with or without cream.

GUAVA SAUCE CAKE

Add 1/4 C sugar to 1 C guava pulp and heat to boiling. Cool.

Cream 1/2 C shortening with 1 C sugar, blend in 1 egg, and beat well. Sift together 1-3/4 C flour, 1/4 t salt, 1 t ea baking soda and cinnamon, 1/2 t cloves, and add to creamed mixture. Blend in puree mixture and beat until smooth. Add 1/2 C ea raisins and chopped nuts.

Pour into 8-in square pan and bake in 350 oven 35-40 mins.

Guava pulp should be consistency of apple sauce. If too thick, thin with guava or similar fruit juice.

LYCHEES

The reddish-shelled lychees with their sweet, juicy, white flesh covering a small brown seed were imported from China in 1873. You can find them in the market in June and July.

If you freeze lychees, be sure to leave 2 in of stem on the fruit so as not to expose the flesh. However, the best way to eat them is freshly picked.

Substitute lychees for grapes when cooking chicken or fish dishes. Add to a fruit or chicken salad and fruit cocktail.

For a pupu, stuff pitted lychees with cream cheese combined with either chopped preserved ginger in syrup or chopped macadamia nuts.

For dessert, peel them and top with creme de menthe and garnish with mint.

CHICKEN LYCHEE

Brown 1 sliced onion in 4 T salad oil for 5 mins, add 4 lbs floured chicken parts, 1 C fresh lychees, and 2 C chicken stock. Cover tightly and cook very slowly for 1 hr.

MOUNTAIN APPLES

This fruit grows wild in rainy valleys, and the fragile fruit, with its red or white skin, tastes best eaten off the tree. Sometimes you can find them for sale at roadside stands during the summer.

For a delicious pie, substitute mountain apple slices for the apple.

Because of the large amount of water and delicate flavor, it is a great addition to salads and cocktails. Cut in half, remove the seed, and slice or cube. There isn't enough pectin or flavor, however, to make into jelly or preserves.

STRAWBERRY GUAVA

This small, round fruit measuring 1 to 2-1/2 inches in diameter is sweeter and has a more delicate flavor than the common guava. The fruit ripens to a deep purplish-red, and the skin is easily bruised. In comparison with the common guava, the strawberry guava has twice as much calcium and is best enjoyed eaten fresh.

STRAWBERRY GUAVA JUICE

Use only the firm, ripe fruit. Wash, cut off blossom ends, and slice in half into a large kettle. Fill with water to barely below the fruit and boil until very soft, about 20 mins. Empty into jelly bag and hang to drip, but do not squeeze bag if you want a clear liquid. Use to combine with other fruit juices for cool drinks.

STRAWBERRY GUAVA JELLY

Bring 4 C juice to boil in shallow kettle and boil rapidly for 10 mins, then add 3-4 C of sugar, depending on sweetness, and return to boiling point. Let it continue at a rolling boil for 20 mins, remove scum, and test frequently until it sheets from the spoon. Pour into hot sterilized jars.

You will find these growing wild in the hills from May to November.

LILIKOI

The song from "My Fair Lady"..."Let a woman in your life"...is quite applicable to the lilikoi or passion fruit vine! Let this wandering tendril with its purplish flower and fruit in your garden, and it will take over your yard!

The 2 to 3-in oval fruit has a hard shell and is either purple or yellow when ripe. Encased in the shell is a highly acidic, juicy pulp full of black seeds.

Gather the lilikoi, wash, hold securely, pierce the shell with a sharp knife, and then slice in half. They tend to slip so be careful. Remove the pulp from the white sac with a spoon, and you can eat it as is or put it through a ricer for the juice.

Sprinkle the pulp with the seeds over a platter of fruit for decoration and flavor.

The juice keeps indefinitely in the refrigerator, and is a good addition to other Island fruits in a punch. It makes excellent pies and jellies.

NANCY VERACRUZ'S EXTRA SPECIAL LILIKOI PIE

Crust: In a bowl combine 1-1/2 C flour, 2 T wheat germ, 2 T chopped walnuts or macadamia nuts, and 3/4 t salt. Cut in 1/2 C shortening (Crisco and 1/2 oleo). Gradually add 2 to 3 T water to blend, and form into ball.

Roll out between 2 sheets of floured wax paper, place in 9-inch pie plate, and bake in 475 oven for 8 to 10 mins.

Filling: sprinkle 1 package unflavored gelatin slowly into 1/4 C water to soak. Cook in double boiler: 1/2 C lilikoi juice, 1/2 t salt, 1/2 C sugar, and 4 egg yolks. Stir constantly until thick, then add the gelatin. Let this cool.

Beat 4 egg whites and slowly add 1/2 C sugar until it holds a peak. Fold into thoroughly cooled lilikoi mixture and pour into baked pie shell. Refrigerate 3 to 4 hrs and add whipped cream at serving time!

NATSUKO TERAMOTO'S LILIKOI JELLY

Bring 3 C sugar and 1 C water to a boil, and boil hard for 1 min. Remove from stove, add 1 bag of Certo, and mix well. Add 1/2 C lilikoi juice, skim, and pour jelly into sterilized jars.

VIRGINIA SIEWERTSEN'S SUPER LILIKOI BARS

Heat oven to 350 and lightly grease a 9x9-in baking pan.

Combine the following, mix well and press into pan: 1 C flour, 1/4 C powdered sugar, and 1/2 C soft butter or oleo. Bake for 12-15 mins.

While this is baking, mix the filling: combine 2 slightly beaten eggs, 3 T fresh lilikoi juice, pinch of salt, 1 C sugar, 1 T cornstarch, and 1/2 t baking powder. Mix well, pour over hot crust, and continue baking another 25 minutes.

Cool this in the refrigerator, then frost with the following: combine 3/4 C sifted powdered sugar with 1 T oleo or butter and 2 T fresh lilikoi juice. If it is too thick for spreading consistency, add a drop more of the juice to correct. Let it set, then cut into bars.

FATHER'S DAY

Surprise him! Give him a new grill, and while you're at it, dress him up with a chef's hat and special apron with pockets filled with all new utensils needed to tend the grill. As a piece de resistance, allow him to try out his new toys on a specially ordered juicy steak.

TIPS ON GRILLING STEAKS

Before grilling steaks, sprinkle with brandy and let sit about 15 mins.

S&P meat after grilling.

Grill a 1-in sirloin steak 10-12 mins for rare and 14-16 mins for medium.

TERIYAKI STEAK MARINADE

Combine 1 C ea soy and raw sugar, 1/4 C sauterne, 1 mashed clove garlic, 1 t ginger, minced, and pour over steaks to marinate for 1-2 hrs.

BUTTERFLIED LEG OF LAMB

Marinate 1 5-6 lb butterflied leg of lamb in following sauce: 1 C red wine, 3/4 C soy, 6-8 crushed cloves garlic, 1 T rosemary, and 1 t thyme. Seal in plastic bag, refrigerate for 6 hrs, turning often.

When coals are ready in grill, drain the meat, reserving the marinade, and grill lamb 4 inches above coals about 25 mins on each side. Check the lamb for doneness frequently until done to your preference.

BARBECUED SPARERIBS

Boil 3-4 lbs spareribs in salted water for 1 hr the day before, and soak overnight in following marinade: cook together for 1/2 hr 1/2 C oil, 3/4 C ketchup, 3 T sugar, 1 T Worcestershire Sauce, 2 T prepared mustard, 2 t salt, and 1/2 t pepper.

Barbecue over low coals 15 mins on each side until nicely browned.

BARBECUE CHICKEN

Cut 1-1/2 - 2 lb young fryers in half and butter well. Grill over coals, inner side first and skin side last. Baste frequently with melted butter and lemon juice or your favorite marinade.

GRILLED LAMB CHOPS

As a really special treat, have your butcher prepare lamb chops cut 1-in thick. Season with S&P, thyme, garlic powder, and rosemary to taste. When the coals are hot, dip chops in melted butter and sear quickly on each side. Spread coals to lower heat and continue cooking 15 mins, turning once or twice, or until done to your liking. Remove to heated platter and serve with baked bananas, buttered Chinese peas or baby string beans.

Options: drizzle green creme de menthe sparingly over chops for just a hint of mint, or top each chop with a dollop of warmed mango chutney and spread thinly over meat.

Koloa Sugar Mill   *Courtesy of Mr. Phillip Scott*

JULY

◆

July is Fireworks
For Freedom!

It's Picnic Time! Join the celebration with America's favorites...Hot Dogs, Hamburgers and Ice Cream. Then drift through the rest of the month on a variety of Cold Salads and Chicken. Breadfruit may be an acquired taste, but try it again...you might just love it! Pineapples are at the peak of their season!

PICNICS

Why do meals taste so much better in the great outdoors...with all the birds, bees, and ants! Maybe it's because it's a great respite from the usual routine, but it's still a good idea to make a list and check it before leaving home.

Keep a handy picnic basket or even a cardboard box ready for a moment's notice, and replenish the paper plates and napkins, and plastic cups and utensils after each use. Suggested inventory besides the aforementioned: trash bags, corkscrew with bottle opener, can opener, flashlight, oil cloth tablecloth, chopsticks, matches in plastic bag, small S&P shakers, cutting knives, peanut butter, mini mustard and catsup sacks, and a jar of Hawaiian salt.

Concentrate on the ice supply for the coolers. To avoid food poisoning, keep cold foods really cold and hot food hot. Don't ever eat leftovers from a picnic unless they have been kept really cold at all times.

Mayonnaise can be the villain at any picnic, especially combined with foods that are left in the sun.

It's a good idea to prepare everything at home the day before the picnic so as to adequately chill the food before packing in ice-filled coolers the next day.

Use your imagination! Make the food interesting, different, delicious, and have something special that they don't get every day.

Work your menu around a Baked Ham. It's a good choice for many reasons: you can take it pre-cooked to the picnic, it's easy to slice, everyone likes ham, and it offers many options.

Begin with a Dagwood ham sandwich and choose from a variety of breads, pita bread, or rolls. Then on to a line-up of mayonnaise, sliced cheeses, tomatoes, onions, avocados, lettuce or sauerkraut, sprouts, hot and mild mustards, horseradish, and chutney.

For starters while the gang gathers, serve a delicious icy cold soup such as **CHILLED WATERCRESS SOUP.**

In blender container add 2 cans potato soup, grated onion to taste, 1 bunch cleaned, chopped watercress, 2 t or more curry, tabasco, and Worcestershire sauce, and S&P to taste. Add half-and-half to consistency you prefer while blending. Check seasoning, chill, and serve very cold.

Potato Salad is a natural with ham, and this **NEW POTATO SALAD** is great as it contains no mayonnaise.

Boil up 16-20 halved, small, new red potatoes until tender, and combine with 1 jar artichoke hearts, quartered.

Dressing: In blender container combine 1 C oil, 1/4 C white wine vinegar, 2 T coarsely chopped fresh basil, 1/2 C finely chopped green onions including greens, 1/4 C round red onions, chopped, 1 t Dijon mustard, 1 clove garlic, crushed, and S&P to taste. Blend well, pour over salad ingredients, and marinate overnight. Serve really cold, garnished with quartered eggs and crisp lettuce leaves.

Make up a batch of **BAKED BEANS**. They go well with ham, too. Heat in oven and wrap casserole securely in newspaper before you leave the house, and they should stay warm enough.

To a 12-oz can of Boston Baked Beans add 3 strips bacon, fried and chopped, 1/3 C dry sherry, 2 T brown sugar, and 1 t ea dry mustard and instant coffee. Stir to blend flavors and pour into bean pot. Bake in 275 oven for about 40 mins to an hr, or until beans begin bubbling.

Spread out a **SALAD BAR**.

Fill bowls, dishes, or platters with: diced celery, chopped green onions, strips of green, yellow and red bell peppers, sliced radishes, fresh small mushrooms, and shredded carrots. Add mini beets, cherry tomatoes, cauliflower flowerettes, and sliced cucumbers. End with crispy lettuce, alfalfa sprouts, and shredded red and green cabbage.

Line up at least three kinds of dressings and provide each guest with a large bowl so he can mix his own salad.

Set out a large platter of cold cuts and cheese or bowls of fresh shrimp, seafood, or chicken salad mix and pink hard boiled eggs.

FRANKFURTERS

What's better than a hot dog? A second hot dog with more relish, more mustard, and an icy beer!

If you poach franks before grilling them, they keep juicier and are more tender. Cover franks with boiling water, cover, and leave handy to grill so they can be thrown over the coals and briefly browned on all sides.

Then pass the relish, horseradish, ketchup, mustard, and mayo!

FRANKS IN BARBECUE SAUCE

Saute 1/2 C chopped onion in 2 T oil until lightly browned. Add: 1/4 t salt and dash of pepper, 1 T Worcestershire sauce, 1 T ea brown sugar and mustard, 1/2 C ketchup, and 1 T ea sweet pickle relish and vinegar.

Simmer for 5 mins, then add franks and heat thoroughly. Split buns, toast on grill, and fill with franks and sauce. Good for 6 franks.

HOT DOGS WITH BAKED BEANS

Spread bottom of hot dog bun with mayonnaise and mustard.

Drain can of pork and beans well and flavor with minced onions, Worcestershire sauce, brown sugar and mustard, dash of lemon juice, and flavor with garlic salt. Spread beans on bottom bun, add frank, cover top with roll, wrap in foil, and grill to heat through.

FRANKS AND CHEESE

Toast halved rolls and insert split frank, add mustard and slice of cheese. Wrap in foil and grill till cheese is melted.

COLESLAW goes well with hot dogs.

Shred enough cabbage for 3 C. Peel, core, and cut 3 apples into strips and sprinkle with lemon juice. Combine cabbage and apple in large salad bowl.

In separate bowl crumble 1/4 lb blue cheese and add 1 T vinegar, 3 T grated cheddar cheese, 1 T minced chives, 2 T chopped green onions, 1 t salt, 1/2 t pepper, and combine well with 1 C sour cream. Pour over the slaw and toss well. Chill well.

SPUR OF THE MOMENT PICNIC

This can be a do-it-yourself, fun picnic! Grab your ever-ready picnic basket and pack bread, saloon pilots, jar of mayonnaise, a lemon, can of either crab meat, salmon or sardines, sliced cheese, and well rinsed and dried lettuce. To be on the safe side, add a jar of peanut butter and jelly. Add some nuts and apples and you can be off!

BASIC OLD STYLE HAWAIIAN PICNIC

Old-timers were ready to go off on a picnic anytime, and food was no problem. From the icebox they took a jar of quartered raw onions in vinegar, a bottle of Chili Pepper Water, and any limu there was. From the counter they took their tin of poi, and from the larder they took cans of salmon, lunch tongue, sardines, or corn beef.

More than likely someone always caught enough fish and they gathered plenty of opihis to have a real feast after their swim!

SALADS

GREEN SALAD

Wash lettuce or watercress or both, dry thoroughly, and break up. Place in a large chilled bowl and sprinkle with salt and fresh ground pepper.

Fry chopped slices of bacon until very crisp and sprinkle this over greens. Rinse pan with vinegar and pour over salad. Serve immediately.

CREAMY COLESLAW

Shred 1/2 head medium size cabbage and chill. Combine 1/2 C cream or yogurt, 2 T vinegar, 1/2 t salt, 1/8 t pepper, and 2 T sugar. Shake well and toss with cabbage, sprinkle with paprika, and serve cold.

Options: add chopped green pepper, shredded carrots, skinned and chopped broccoli stems, 1 t celery seed, and prepared mustard to dressing.

HOT CHICKEN SALAD

Marinate 2 C cooked chicken cut in bite-size chunks in French dressing for an hour. Drain and combine with 2 C diagonally cut celery, 2 T minced onion, 1/2 jar capers, 1/2 C mayonaise, S&P, 1 can sliced water chestnuts, and 1/2 C coarsely chopped macadamia nuts. Turn into 1-1/2 qt casserole and top with 1/2 C grated Swiss cheese and 1 C crushed potato chips. Bake in 350 oven for 30 mins till cheese melts.

HOT CHICKEN SALAD #2

Combine 1 C cut-up cooked chicken, 2 T ea slivered celery, minced onion, chopped green pepper, sliced almonds, lemon juice, and parsley, 1 6-oz can mushroom pieces, 2 t salt, dash pepper, and 1 C mayonnaise. Mix thoroughly and add more mayonnaise if too dry.

In casserole place a layer of lightly toasted bread cubes in bottom, spoon chicken mixture over cubes, and top with cubed bread. Slightly beat 2 eggs with 1-1/2 C milk and pour over all. Refrigerate overnight. Pour can cream of mushroom soup over mixture, top with croutons and Parmesan cheese, and bake in 325 oven for 1 hour. If you have any leftover ham available, chop and add to mixture, too.

GRANDMA GROSSMUTIER'S WARM POTATO SALAD

Boil 6 new or small white potatoes, peel and slice fairly thin, and place in a bowl. Fry 6 or more slices of bacon until crisp and drain. Cook 1/3 C ea chopped onion and celery in bacon fat just for a min, add 2 T flour, 2 T or less of sugar, 1-1/2 t salt, 1/2 t caraway seed, dash of pepper, and stir in gradually 3/4 C water and 1/2 C vinegar. Slowly cook until mixture boils for 1 min. Pour over spuds in bowl, add some bacon, cover, and let stand until ready to serve. When ready, heat over hot water, remove to lettuce lined bowl, garnish with remaining bacon and if you like, chives. Serves 6.

Make this a day or so in advance to let it marinate in refrigerator until an hour before serving, then warm. Good with ham.

PEA SALAD

Thaw 2 packages frozen tiny peas, drain, and combine with 1 C sour cream or plain yogurt, 5 slices fried bacon, crumbled, 1/2 C ea chopped celery hearts and green onions, and add 1 C chopped macadamia nuts. Chill well and serve cold.

Instead of adding chopped green onions, add chopped mint.

MINTED BEAN SALAD

Steam 1 lb fresh green beans till tender, immediately blanch in ice water, and drain well on paper towels. Toss beans with 1 C ea chopped red onion, coarsely chopped toasted walnuts, and crumbled feta cheese.

Toss with dressing 1/2 hr before serving. Mix together in food processor or blender: 1 C packed (2 or 3 bunches) fresh mint leaves (take leaves off stem, rinse under cold water, spin in salad spinner to dry), 2-3 cloves garlic, 1/3 C white wine vinegar, 1/4 to 1/2 t salt, 1/4 to 1/2 t pepper, and 3/4 C good olive oil. Blend well. Serve salad cold.

POTATO SALAD

Scrub a dozen small, red, new potatoes and boil until just tender. Test them gently with a fork so as not to break them. Drain and cut in quarters. While potatoes are still hot, add 3 T chopped parsley, 2 T fresh dill or 2 t dry dill, 6 T ea chopped celery and green onions, and 1 large green pepper, chopped. Mix thoroughly and toss with dressing.

Dressing: mix together 1/3 C red wine vinegar, 3/4 C olive oil, 2 t mustard, and 1 clove garlic, crushed. Sprinkle with freshly ground pepper.

TOMATO ASPIC MOLDS

Heat 1 11-oz can condensed tomato soup to boiling, remove from heat, add 1 large package cream cheese, and beat with hand beater until blended. Add 1 envelope unflavored gelatin that has been dissolved in 1/4 C water.

Cool, but don't allow to thicken. Add 1 C mayonnaise, 1 C finely chopped celery, 4 stalks chopped green onions, 1/2 chopped green pepper, and 2 sliced pimentos. Stir and mix well and pour into molds or large bowl to chill until firm. Serve on beds of lettuce with or without sliced avocados and dressing.

COBB SALAD

Toss together: 2 C diced avocado, 2 C diced tomatoes, 2 diced hard-boiled eggs, 2 C diced chicken or turkey, 1/2 C crisp, drained, and crumbled bacon, 2 T minced fresh chives, S&P to taste, and serve on shredded greens. 4 servings.

Garnish with parsley, red radishes, and ripe olives on the side.

Blue cheese or ranch dressing may be served along with hot rolls.

BLUE CHEESE DRESSING

Mix by hand until fluffy: 1 clove minced garlic, 2 T sugar, 1/3 C sour cream, 2-1/2 C real mayonnaise, and fold in 1-1/2 C coarsely crumbled blue cheese (about 1/2 lb) into mixture. 1 qt.

GREEN GODDESS DRESSING

Combine 1 C mayonnaise, 1 clove garlic, minced, 3 chopped anchovies, 1/4 C chopped parsley, 1 T fresh lemon juice, 1 T tarragon vinegar, 1/2 t salt, and coarsely ground black pepper to taste. Blend well, then fold in 1/2 C sour cream, whipped. Pour over tossed green salad.

STAN'S SPECIAL SALAD DRESSING

Put an egg in hot water for 1 min and remove.

Combine the following ingredients and blend with a wire whisk: 1/4 C lemon juice, 1/2 to 3/4 C olive oil, 1 t Worcestershire sauce, squirt of anchovy paste, 1 clove crushed garlic, 1 t salt, dash of pepper, and the egg. When well blended, refrigerate. Pour over cleaned, dried, and broken-up Romaine lettuce, croutons, and freshly grated Parmesan cheese.

HONEY DRESSING

Mix together 1/3 C ea sugar and honey, 1 t ea dry mustard and paprika, 1/4 t salt, 6 T vinegar, 2 T lemon juice and 1/3 t grated onion. Slowly pour in 1 C salad oil, beating constantly. Makes 2 cups.

This is good with a fruit salad.

CHICKEN

Rub a roasting chicken inside and out with a cut lemon. It enhances the flavor.

ALICE'S SWEET SOUR CHICKEN WINGS

Cut 3 lbs chicken wings into 3 parts, boil tips of wings for soup stock. Sprinkle garlic powder and salt over chicken and leave for 1/2 hr. Dip chicken in 2 beaten eggs, then in potato starch, and fry until they turn light brown.

Glaze: boil 1/2 C ea sugar, soup stock, and Japanese vinegar, 3 T ea ketchup and soy, and pour over wings. Bake at 350 until done, basting once while baking. Chicken is done when glaze has thickened.

CREAMY CHICKEN HASH

Combine 1 C light cream and 2 t flour, add 1 C ea cooked chicken, coarsely cut mushrooms sauteed in butter, 1/2 t grated lemon rind, S&P to taste, and 1 t grated onion. Cook over low heat, stirring constantly until thickened. Divide 2 C cooked flat noodles in 4 individual casseroles, pour mixture over, sprinkle with grated Parmesan cheese, and brown 5 in from broiler.

SADIE'S COLD OR HOT CHICKEN DINNER

Rub a roasting chicken with juice of 1 lemon and place onion in cavity. Roast with margarine or butter in 350 oven until tender. Cool, remove meat from bones, and make sauce.

Sauce: combine 1 glass white wine, 2 T ea honey, fruit chutney, and curry, and simmer 20-25 mins. Cool and add 1/4 pt ea cream and mayonnaise. Toss with chicken pieces and sprinkle with chopped parsley. If serving cold, decorate the platter with bunches of grapes or fresh fruit.

If Sadie serves this hot, she often uses only leg or thigh pieces.

CHICKEN BALLS IN CONSOMME

Combine 1 lb minced or ground chicken with 4 small onions, chopped fine, 3 dried mushrooms, soaked and chopped fine, 1 piece grated ginger, dash of chili powder, 1 egg, 1-1/4 t salt and mold into balls 1-in diameter.

Bring 6 C rich, homemade chicken stock to boil, reduce heat, add chicken balls, and let them simmer in the stock. Remove the balls when they float to the surface, but don't over-boil. Season to taste. Add sprigs of Chinese parsley or chopped watercress and the balls. Serve piping hot in soup bowls.

CHICKEN CURRY

Steam a 3-4 lb roaster or broiler until tender, remove skin, de-bone meat, and cut into bite-size pieces. Cover and put aside. Throw carcass and large bones back in pot with water to cover, and simmer an hour for broth. You will need 2 C chicken stock.

In large pot, melt 6 T butter or oleo, add 1 large minced onion, 1 sliced stalk celery, 1 peeled and chopped green apple, and 6 cloves minced garlic. Cook over low heat until veggies are limp.

Combine 1/2 C flour, 2-3 T curry, 1 t ea dry mustard and paprika, S&P to taste, and dash of cayenne pepper. Sprinkle mixture over onions and stir over low heat until blended. Slowly add 1-1/4 C broth and 1 C light cream and stir until smooth. Add more stock if too thick.

This apple flavor is a change from coconut milk.

Serve with condiments: chopped hard-boiled eggs, chopped peanuts, chutney, chopped crispy bacon, chopped green onions, and shredded fresh coconut.

CRANBERRY-ORANGE CHICKEN
is good "fingerlickin" picnic fare.

Bake 4 lbs chicken pieces 15 mins, skin side down, and turn. While chicken is baking, combine 14-oz can of whole cranberry sauce in a pot with 1/4 C each orange juice concentrate and soy and 1/3 C honey. Bring to a boil, lower heat, and simmer 5 mins. Pour sauce over chicken and bake 1-1/2 hrs in 375 oven. Turn pieces every so often to make sure they are evenly coated. The longer you bake, the stickier it will get.

RABBIT

RABBIT HASENPFEFFER

Place 1 cut-up fryer rabbit in glass bowl.

Marinade: combine 1 C cider vinegar, 1-1/2 C water, 2 t ea onion salt and brown sugar, 1/4 t pepper, 1 t whole cloves, 6 bay leaves, and 1 C sliced onion. Pour over meat and refrigerate overnight.

Next day remove fryer from liquid, drain and save liquid, roll pieces in flour, and brown in 1/8 in hot fat. Add marinade, turn down heat, cover tightly, and simmer 1 hr or until tender. Stir in mixture of flour and water to thicken gravy.

MICHELE FERGUSON'S LAPIN
AU POUILLY FUISSE (Rabbit Stew)

Cut up 3 dressed rabbits. Fry 1 lb diced bacon and 50 pearl onions in 1/2 stick butter until slightly golden, remove, and saute rabbit a few pieces at a time. Flambe with 1/4 C brandy, sprinkle with flour, and add 3 C white wine, dry Pouilly Fuisse, 2 T red wine vinegar, 4 C chicken stock, thyme, bay leaf, and parsley to taste, 12 peppercorns, and 2 cloves garlic, quartered.

Simmer for 15 mins, add bacon mixture, and simmer for 15 mins longer. Add 16-ozs fresh mushrooms, quartered, stir in 4 T Dijon mustard, and simmer another 15 mins.

Sprinkle with parsley and serve with a potato dish...sweet potatoes recommended. Serves 20.

FRUIT

BREADFRUIT

This versatile fruit is available usually between July and February. It was most probably brought to Hawaii from Tahiti by the early settlers. When picked, the rind of mature fruit is yellowish-green and still hard, but it softens within 24 to 36 hrs if picked properly. The immature fruit is pea green in color.

You may either leave the core in when baking or remove it. Bake in the oven with a pan of water for steam, thereby creating an imu-like condition.

To bake a fully ripe breadfruit, remove stem and core by cutting, twisting, and pulling, and line the cavity with Hawaiian salt. Let it stand about 3 hrs. When ready to cook, add several dollops of butter in the cavity, place in a baking pan, and bake in 350 oven until tender...about 1-2 hrs until really soft.

Breadfruit, boiled until tender, can be cut in cubes and added to stews instead of potatoes, or used in salads like potato.

Add cooked cubes to a clear soup.

Mash baked breadfruit with butter and S&P. Make into patties, and fry until golden brown.

BREADFRUIT PUPU

Boil 4 C diced, peeled, green breadfruit for an hour, or until tender, in 3 C salted water. Drain and cool. Serve with a flavored mayonnaise dip.

Or serve this hot as a dinner starch seasoned with S&P, nutmeg and butter. Tastes just like artichoke hearts.

BREADFRUIT BREAD

Cream 2/3 C vegetable shortening and 1-1/4 C sugar, beat in 3 eggs, then 2 C mashed, cooked breadfruit.

Combine 1 C white flour and 2 C whole wheat flour, 4 t baking powder, 1/2 t baking soda, and 1 t salt. Add flour mixture alternately with 1/2 C milk. Add 1/4 t lemon extract and large handful of raisins. Turn into greased loaf pan, bake in 350 oven 1 hr and 20 mins. For 2 small loaves, bake 1 hr.

BREADFRUIT CHIPS
have a unique flavor all their own.

To make them, skin a mature green breadfruit and slice the flesh as thin as possible using an electric slicer if possible. Soak slices in salted water, dry thoroughly, and fry in deep fat. Drain on paper towels, salt, and store in air tight jars or freeze.

BREADFRUIT SALAD

Marinate cubes of 1 cooked, mature green breadfruit cut in 3/4 in cubes in French dressing.

In a bowl combine: 1 C celery, chopped, 1 C won bok, finely sliced, 1/2 C green onions, sliced, 2 hard boiled eggs, sliced, 1/2 C macadamia nuts, chopped, 1 T Worcestershire sauce, and combine with breadfruit. Add S&P to taste and fold in enough mayonnaise to moisten well. Taste to correct seasoning. Serve chilled on lettuce leaves.

PINEAPPLE

Usually available all year round, but they are abundant in June, July, and August.

To pick a good fruit, see that the crown is small and well formed. It is well ripened if a snap produces a dull, solid sound.

Pineapples may be served in slices alone or mixed with other fruits in salads, cocktails or juice. Slices of pineapple are delicious in iced tea. They may be preserved in jams or pickles, but don't have enough pectin to make jelly.

Prepare pineapple chunks or slices and mix with lots of freshly chopped mint. Keep well covered in refrigerator.

Add fresh or canned pieces of pineapple to a creamy coleslaw.

Use the shell for boats to hold fruit salads.

Pineapple combines well with avocado.

PINEAPPLE CHUTNEY

Combine 2 C cider vinegar, 2 C brown sugar, 1 clove mashed garlic, 4 small, dried hot chili peppers, crushed and seeded, 1 T finely chopped fresh ginger, 1 t ea salt and whole cloves, and 1-1/2 C raisins or currants in a large 4-6 qt pan. Bring to a boil. Add 12 C peeled, cored, diced, fresh pineapple, return to a boil, and simmer about an hr or until pineapple is tender and syrup is thick. Jar in sterilized containers.

PINEAPPLE PICKLE

Cut cored pineapple in about 1-in wide sections. Combine 12 C fruit with 3 C white vinegar, 3-1/2 C sugar, and 3 C water, and add bag containing 2 T whole cloves and 2 sticks of cinnamon. Boil slowly for 15 mins, turn down heat, and boil gently with cover on for 1-1/2 hrs or until tender. Pour into sterilized jars and seal.

NOTES

Puolu

Courtesy of Mrs. Thurmond Clarke

AUGUST

*It's August and the lethargy
of summer is beginning to be
a way of life!*

With the long days, it's an opportune time to fill the larder with Preserves and keep the Cookie jar filled for points. Cool off with icy Cold Soups.

PRESERVES

IRENE'S GUESS WHAT MARMALADE

Place 2 C finely chopped cucumber in large saucepan, add 4 C sugar, 1/3 C lime juice, 2 T grated lime peel, and mix well. Place over high heat, bring to full rolling boil for exactly 1 min, stirring constantly. Remove from heat and add 1/2 bottle Certo at once. Skim off foam, then stir and skim for 5 mins to cool slightly and prevent floating cucumber bits. Pour into sterilized jars. 2 pts.

LU REYNOLDS'
BREAD AND BUTTER PICKLES

Sprinkle 1 C Hawaiian salt over 6 qts sliced cucumbers, add ice cubes, and mix. Let stand 3 hrs, then rinse cukes. In a large pot combine with 12 medium onions, sliced, 4 large green peppers, sliced, 1/4 C mustard seed, 2 T celery seed, 2 t tumeric powder, 10 C sugar, and 2-1/2 qts vinegar. Bring just to boiling point, stir, and pour in sterilized jars.

LU'S CONGEE

Combine 3 lbs prunes, 12 lemons, sliced, 2 T sugar, and 4 T salt. Turn into large bottle and leave in sun for 1 week.

CRISPY TANGY VEGGIES

Cut 1 lb peeled carrots in strips or bite-size pieces. Slice a cauliflower in bite sizes. Boil 1-1/2 T salt in enough water to blanch vegetables 1 min. Drain, rinse, and pack in pt jars.

In a pot combine 1 C cider vinegar, 1-1/4 C water, 1/4 C sugar, 2 crushed garlic buds, 1-1/2 t dill, and 1 t salt. Bring to boil to dissolve sugar, cool, and pour over veggies. Keep refrigerated.

VEGETABLES IN MARINADE

Combine 4 C assorted fresh vegetables, peeled and sliced, (jicama, zucchini, quartered Maui onions, cauliflower, carrots) and jar.

In another large jar combine 1 minced clove garlic, 1 C Japanese vinegar, 1 t sugar, 1/4 t dried mustard, 1/2 t salt, 1/4 t black pepper, and if you want it really hot, 1 Hawaiian red chili pepper, seeded and chopped. Correct seasoning to taste, shake well to blend, and pour over vegetables. Cover and refrigerate overnight. Shake jar occasionally to coat all vegetables with marinade. Can be refrigerated up to 5 days.

APPLE CHUTNEY

In a large pot combine: 8 cored, unpeeled, and chopped tart apples with 2-1/4 C brown sugar, 1-1/3 C cider vinegar, 2 cloves minced garlic, 1 thumb ginger, grated or finely minced, and 1 large chopped onion.

Cook gently for 45 mins or until fairly thick. Add 2 C raisins, 1 t ea salt, ginger and mustard seed, 1/8 t cayenne or small, finely chopped, de-seeded Hawaiian chili peppers or Tabasco sauce to taste. Check seasoning and cook another 30 mins or until thick. Jar in sterilized containers. Makes 4 C.

FRANCES FRAZIER'S ELECTRIC FRYING PAN JAM

This takes much less time than conventional methods.

PINEAPPLE PAPAYA JAM

Pare and core one pineapple and put through slicer blade of food processor. Pare, seed, and slice enough papayas to make equivalent amount of pulp. (Drain any juice and reserve for drinking.)

Add a cup-for-cup of pulp and sugar and turn into electric frying pan. Cook until thick. Jar in sterilized containers.

ENGLISH STYLE PICKLED ONIONS

Keeps a month in refrigerator.

In a large bowl, stir 1/2 C salt with 3 C cold water until dissolved and add 2 lbs small white boiling onions, peeled. Cover and refrigerate for 12 to 24 hrs.

Drain onions, cover with cold water, drain again, and pack in a wide-mouth 1-1/2 qt jar or crock or 3 1-pint jars. In a saucepan stir together 2 C white vinegar, 1/4 C dark brown sugar, firmly packed, 1 t each allspice, mustard seed, whole black pepper, and mixed pickling spice; bring to

boiling. Pour hot marinade over onions. Let cool, cover, and refrigerate for at least a week before serving.

MARTHA JUDD'S PICKLED ONIONS

Bring 1 C Hawaiian salt and 5 C water to boil, cool, and strain. Pour over 2 lbs sliced onions, with 2 bay leaves, 12 peppercorns, and 2 Hawaiian red peppers, or more if you want, cover, and let stand 24 hrs. Drain, mix 1 C water, 1 C cider vinegar, and 2 T sugar, and pour over onions. Refrigerate for 3 days before eating.

HELEN F. NICHOLS' MOCK STRAWBERRY RELISH

This is good with fowl, pork, or lamb.

Mix well 1-1/2 C ground raw cranberries, 1-1/2 C ground raw apples (cooking apple such as Pippins, about 4 or 5, peeled), 1 flat can crushed pineapple, drained (or fresh), and 1-1/2 C sugar. Freeze in plastic containers. The food processor works well for this.

MILDRED MEAD'S CRANBERRY CHUTNEY

In a large deep saucepan combine 4 C whole cranberries with 2-1/2 C sugar, 1 C water, 6 whole cloves, 2 cinnamon sticks, and 1/2 t salt. Bring to a boil, stirring frequently. Cook 10 mins or until berries pop. Add 1 C light raisins, 2 tart apples and pears, peeled, cored and diced, 1 small onion, chopped, and 1/2 C sliced celery.

Continue stirring and cooking until thick, about 15 mins. Remove from heat and stir in 1/2 C chopped walnuts and 1 t lemon zest. Ladle into sterilized jars and process in boiling water for 10 mins. (2 qts.)

If you like it hot, add some minced or grated ginger to taste.

KIM CHEE

Cut up cabbage (preferably won bok), daikon, de-seeded cucumbers, and mix all together. Sprinkle with Hawaiian salt and let stand about 2-3 hrs. Put veggies in qt bottle and add 2 T packaged Kim Chee mix, 1 C water, sliced garlic, and dash of Aji. Let stand at least 2 days before indulging.

HARRIET WARREN'S GINGER PEACHES

Drain a 29-oz can peach halves. Combine 3/4 C syrup with 1/2 C cider vinegar, add 1 C light-brown sugar and 1 t ground ginger. Simmer 5 mins, add peaches, and simmer 5 mins longer. Chill and serve with any entree.

A few apricots may be added for color.

CHILI PEPPER WATER #1

Carefully wash an appropriate amount of chili peppers and garlic cloves. Chop fine and add salt and water. Boil for 10 mins, remove from heat, and pour into clean container. Do not use defective jars with chipped edges or paper-lined lids.

Add at least 1 T of distilled white vinegar per cup of chili pepper water, mix well, and cap. Store in refrigerator immediately and between uses.

CHILI PEPPER WATER #2

Carefully wash an appropriate amount of chili peppers and garlic cloves. Marinate them in vinegar, without water, and store in refrigerator immediately and between uses.

CROCKED FRUIT

Use fresh fruit in season when possible, but canned are acceptable. Cut peaches, plums, seedless grapes, nectarines, apples, and apricots in fairly large pieces. Place equal amount of sugar and fresh fruit that has been peeled and pitted in a large crock. Leave at room temperature for an hour or so. Pour enough brandy, rum, or bourbon over the fruit to cover. Place a lid on the crock and keep in a cool, dry place for at least a week or longer. Stir before spooning out any of the fruit.

COOKIES

AH KAM WONG'S DOUBLE FROSTED BROWNIES

Combine 1/2 C biscuit mix, 3/4 C sugar, 2 beaten eggs, 1 t vanilla, and 2 T butter or oleo, melted, with 2 squares melted unsweetened chocolate. Mix together, pour into 8x8x2 greased and floured pan, and bake 30 mins in 350 oven. Cool.

Combine and beat 1-1/2 C powdered sugar with 1/4 C soft butter or oleo, 1 t vanilla, and 1 T milk or more to spreading consistency. Spread over cooled cake.

Melt 2 squares unsweetened chocolate over low heat, cool, and spread over the top. Refrigerate to harden. Cut into squares - preferably smallish as this is rich!

ELDEAN SCOTT'S SUPER CHOCOLATE CHIP COOKIES

Combine 2 C flour, 1 T baking soda, and 1 t salt. Cream 1 C butter with 1 C brown sugar and 1/2 C granulated sugar until light. Beat in 1 egg and 1 t vanilla until light and fluffy. Stir in flour mixture, add 12-oz package chocolate chips and 1 C chopped nuts.

Shape into 1 in balls or drop by teaspoonfuls on ungreased cookie sheet about 2 in apart. Bake in 350 oven for 12-15 mins until light brown.

ELENA ATKINS' GUAVA COOKIES

Beat 1 C butter with 1-1/2 C sugar until light and fluffy, add 3 eggs one at a time, and beat thoroughly. Stir in 1 C guava puree and 2 T lemon juice. Sift and stir in 5 C flour combined with 1/2 t salt and 4 t baking powder. Add 3/4 C nuts. Drop by spoonfuls on greased cookie sheet. Bake in 375 oven 12 to 15 mins.

REBA DEESE'S SKILLET COOKIES

Melt 1 stick margarine in pan, add 2 beaten eggs, 3/4 C sugar, dash of salt, 1 lb chopped dates, and stir over low heat 10-15 mins. Remove and add 2 C Rice Krispies, 1 C chopped pecans, and 1 t vanilla. When dough is cool enough to handle, shape into balls and drop into bowl of flaked coconut to coat. No baking needed. Makes 40 balls.

LACY OATMEAL COOKIES

Mix together: 1 cube melted butter, 1 C sugar, 1-1/2 C quick rolled oats, 1 beaten egg, 2 T flour, 1 t baking powder, and 1 t vanilla. Drop by 1/2 t on well-greased (Teflon) cookie sheet. Bake in 350 oven about 6-7 min or until slightly brown.

If they stick taking from cookie sheet, return briefly to oven.

RUTH OKIHARA'S ENERGY BARS

Combine 2-1/2 C Rice Krispies with 2 C oats and bake in 200 oven for 1/2 hr or until crispy. Add 1/2 C roasted peanuts.

Over low heat, melt 1/4 C margarine and 1/2 C peanut butter, add a 10-1/2-oz package mini-marshmallows, and stir until melted. Stir in 1 C raisins, 1/4 C toasted sesame seeds, and the cereal mix.

Remove to a 9x14 in pan lined with saran wrap, cover top with another piece of plastic wrap to flatten. Cool, cut in squares, and wrap each bar individually in saran wrap. Store in sealed cans.

ROSA BULNES' SUGAR COOKIES

With an electric mixer blend 1-1/2 C butter with 2/3 C sugar and 2 t vanilla. Add 2 C flour mixed with 1/8 t salt to blend, then add 1/4 C walnut pieces. Drop by spoonfuls on an ungreased cookie sheet and bake 10 mins at 400.

IRENE NOZAKI'S CARROT COOKIES

Cream 1 C shortening, add 2 C flour sifted with 4 T sugar and 1/2 t salt, 1 t vanilla, and 1 C ea finely grated raw carrots and chopped nuts. Form into rolls, chill, slice 1/2 in thick or drop by spoonfuls on cookie sheet and flatten with dampened fork. Bake 10 mins in 375 oven. Roll warm cookies in powdered sugar. 6 dozen.

AUDREY'S COWBOY COOKIES

Cream 2 C sugar and 1 C brown sugar with 2 cubes butter or margarine until fluffy. Beat in 2 beaten eggs and 1 t vanilla. Sift together 2 C flour, 1 t baking soda, and 1/2 t ea salt and baking powder and add to mixture. Stir in 2 C quick oats, 1 package chocolate chips, and 1 C chopped nuts.

It gets hard to stir toward the end, but electric mixer might help. Drop by teaspoonfuls on greased cookie sheet and bake in 375 oven 10-12 mins.

MRS. PERKINS' FAVORITE WALNUT JUMBLES

Cream 1/4 lb butter with 2-1/2 T brown sugar, add 1 C flour and 1/2 t salt, and blend well. Add 2 t vanilla and 1 C finely chopped nuts. Beat together and drop from teaspoon onto cookie sheet and bake 25 mins in 300 oven.

They melt in your mouth, make you long for more, *and* forget all the calories!

HELEN ESKRIDGE'S BUTTERED RUM COOKIES

Cream until light and fluffy 1 C butter, then add 2 C sugar and continue to cream until absorbed thoroughly. Mix in 3 well beaten eggs, 3 T rum, 1 t vanilla, and 1 t finely grated lemon peel. Add 3 C sifted flour a little at a time, mixing well until smooth.

Chill dough until firm. Press through pastry tube, making small cookies. Bake on lightly buttered cookie sheet in oven at 400 for 15 mins, or until lightly browned. About 100 cookies.

For holiday cookies you may add ground nut meats, bits of candied ginger, candied cherries, or touches of colored frosting for festive trays of assorted cookies.

WALNUT WONDERS FROM THE KITCHEN OF PAT PALAMA

Mix 3 oz package of cream cheese with 1 block of butter, minus 1 inch, and cream well. Add 1 C flour and cream all together into dough. Divide into 20 balls. Press into ungreased mini-muffin tins and set aside while you prepare filling.

Filling: mix well 1/2 C sugar, 1 in butter, 1 egg, 1 t vanilla, and 2/3 C chopped walnuts. Spoon into pastry-lined muffin tins, about 1/2 full each. Bake in a 350 oven for 30 mins or until slightly golden brown.

TEA COOKIES

Cream 1/2 C ea butter and margarine with 3/4 C sugar until very fluffy and light. Add 3/4 t vanilla and 1 egg and beat well.

Sift 2-1/2 C flour, 1 t ea salt and baking soda, and blend well into creamed mixture. Form about 1 t of dough into a ball and roll in sesame seeds to coat well. Place on cookie sheet and flatten each cookie with a fork. Bake in 350 oven for 8-10 mins. These cookies don't need to be brown. Allow cookies to cool and you may freeze a portion. 10 dozen.

CEREAL AND CHOCOLATE CHIP COOKIES

Sift together 1-3/4 C flour, 1 t baking powder, and 1/2 t salt.

Cream 1 C oleo with 3/4 C ea granulated and brown sugar, add 2 eggs and 1 t vanilla, and beat well. Stir in dry ingredients and add 2 C oven-crisped rice cereal and 1 6-oz package semi-sweet chocolate chips.

Drop by level T on greased sheet. Bake in 350 oven 10 min or until lightly browned. Cool 1 min, then remove from pan and place on racks. 6 dozen.

MOLASSES SUGAR COOKIES

Melt 3/4 C shortening over low heat and let cool. Add 1 C sugar, 1/4 C molasses, and 1 egg, and mix. Add 2 C flour with 2 t baking powder, 1/2 t ea cloves, ginger, and salt, and 1 t cinnamon. Chill. Form in 1 in balls, roll in granulated sugar, flatten slightly, and place on greased cookie sheet 2 in apart. Bake 10 mins in 375 oven. Makes 48 cookies.

GINGER SNAPS FROM NANCY SHAW'S KITCHEN

Cream 3/4 C shortening with 1 C sugar until fluffy, add 1 beaten egg and 1/4 C dark molasses. Sift together and add: 2 C flour, 1 T ginger, 2 t baking soda, 1 t cinnamon, and 1/2 t salt.

Roll in balls, then in sugar, and bake on greased cookie sheet 10 mins in 375 oven.

GRANOLA SNACK

Measure 1-1/2 C quick oatmeal, 1/2 C ea regular wheat germ, coconut, and chopped nuts, and 1/2 t salt into mixing bowl. Stir to blend, add 2 T oil, and mix thoroughly. Pour in 2/3 C sweetened condensed milk and blend well. Sprinkle a handful of wheat germ on a cookie sheet and gently spread mixture on top.

Bake in 325 oven about 25 mins, checking as it bakes. After the first 10 mins it will begin to brown, so stir on sheet every 10 mins until it is as brown as you like. Cool on pan and store in covered container in refrigerator.

Or omit milk and substitute 1/2 C honey and bake accordingly.

BISCOTTI

Preheat oven to 350.

Cream 1/2 C butter with 3/4 C sugar together until light and fluffy. Beat in 3 eggs one at a time, blend well, and add 1/2 t vanilla.

Sift together 3 C flour, 3 t baking powder, 1/2 t salt, and stir into batter. Fold in 1 T aniseed, 2 T ea grated lemon and orange rind, and 1 C chopped, blanched almonds and blend well.

Divide dough into three parts and shape into long rolls 1-1/2 in diameter. Place each roll on a separate baking sheet, flatten the top slightly, and bake 15 mins.

Remove from oven, cut rolls into 3/4 in slices, lay them cut side down on the baking sheet, and bake 15 mins longer. Cool on a rack. 4 dozen.

COLD SOUPS

GAZPACHO

In blender container combine 3 cans condensed tomato soup, 2 C water, 3 C chopped, seeded, and peeled cucumbers, 2 C chopped green pepper, 1/2 C chopped green onion, 1/4 to 3/4 C red wine vinegar, 1/4 C corn oil, 1 clove garlic, and a handful of parsley. Blend just to mix. Add 1-1/2 C sour cream, 1 t salt, and cayenne pepper to taste. Blend just briefly and chill. Serve with dollops of sour cream and chopped cucumber or chives on top.

This **GAZPACHO SOUP** can be made ahead of time and frozen.

Into the blender container put: 1 C chicken broth, 4 C of canned tomatoes, 1-1/2 cucumber, peeled and de-seeded, 1-1/2 green pepper, chopped, 1 or 2 cloves of garlic, and turn on medium speed till all is blended smoothly.

Blend in another cup of broth, 1/2 C lemon juice, 1/4 C olive oil, and S&P to taste. Let stand in refrigerator for at least 3 hrs. Yields 4-5 servings.

CHILLED HOMEMADE TOMATO SOUP

In blender container combine 4 large, ripe, peeled tomatoes, 4 T ice water, 1 T sugar, 1 sliced white onion, and puree well. You may or may not strain before adding 1 C sour cream. Blend well and refrigerate. Just before serving stir in 1 t grated lemon rind and 2 t lemon juice and stir well. Garnish with dollop of sour cream and sprig of parsley or chopped chives.

AVOCADO SOUP

In blender container add 1 chopped onion, 1/2 bunch chopped watercress, 2 sliced avocados, 1 can consomme, 1 t lime or lemon juice, 1 T curry powder or to taste, dash of garlic salt and pepper and tabasco for zing. Blend to puree and when well blended, add a carton of plain yogurt (or cream) and blend briefly. Refrigerate until icy cold. Garnish with sprigs of watercress and dash of paprika.

WINONA SEARS'S PAPAYA BISQUE

Saute until soft 3 T butter, 1 large onion, minced, and 2 small carrots, sliced. Add 1 medium potato, sliced, 2 C chicken broth, 1 medium green papaya, sliced, and cook, covered, until vegetables are tender. Put in blender on medium speed until just smooth. Return to pan, add 1/2 C half-and-half, S&P to taste, and heat until hot, but don't boil. Refrigerate to serve cold garnished with parsley and sprinkling of paprika or cayenne. Serves 4.

JOHN ALLERTON'S CHILLED CURRIED ZUCCHINI SOUP

Over moderate heat melt 6 T oleo in frying pan, add 2 lbs chopped zucchini and 1 C minced green onions, or

1 whole round onion. Saute for 15 mins until zucchini is soft, but don't let it brown. Add 1 to 2 T curry and cumin to taste. Continue cooking, stirring for 2 mins. Add 2 C chicken broth and bring to boil.

Puree the mixture in small batches in blender, empty into large container, and add 3 C buttermilk and S&P to taste. Chill for at least 6 hrs. When ready to serve, sprinkle with either chopped chives or parsley. Serves 6.

COLD BEET SOUP

Combine and mix 1 1-lb can beets, chopped, including juice, 2 t ea vinegar or lemon juice and sugar, S&P to taste, and dash of ground cloves. Chop briefly in blender and chill well. Before serving, add 1 diced cucumber, chilled, and serve in cold bowls topped with a dollop of sour cream and chopped chives.

BLENDER BORSCHT

Puree 1-1/2 - 1-2/3 C sliced beets (16 oz can), 1/2 C beet juice, and 3/4 C chicken broth in blender. Add 1-1/2 T lemon juice, 1 heaping T chopped onion, and 1/2 t salt and blend until smooth. Add 2 T sour cream and blend very briefly. Chill at least 6 hrs to develop flavors. Serve garnished with sour cream and chopped chives. 1 qt.

SYBIL DEAN'S VICHYSSOISE SOUP

In large pan brown 1 medium white onion, chopped, and 4-6 leeks, sliced, using white part only, in 1/4 C plus of butter until transparent. Add 6 medium potatoes, peeled and thinly sliced, 1 qt chicken broth, and 2 t salt. Boil 30-40 mins or until tender.

Place in food blender and process on puree, return mixture to pan, add 3 C milk and 1 C cream. Bring to a boil, cool, and rub through sieve. Correct seasoning and chill. Add another cup of cream, stir well, and serve icy cold garnished with finely chopped chives and parsley. Serves 6-8.

GLADYS MINCHIN'S CARROT VICHYSSOISE

Combine 1 medium peeled and diced potato, 1-1/4 C sliced carrots, 3 sliced leeks, white part only, and 3 C chicken broth, and simmer 25 mins or until tender.

In blender, puree half the mixture at a time at high speed for 30 seconds. Pour into pitcher and stir in pinch of white pepper, 1 t ea salt and sugar, and 1 C half-and-half. If too thick, add more half-and-half. Chill. Top with shredded raw carrots or chopped parsley to serve.

TOMATO VICHYSSOISE

Make mashed potatoes according to directions on package of instant potato soup, or make from scratch. Saute 1/4 C minced green onions in a little of 3 C of tomato juice or V-8 Juice, simmer briefly and add potatoes, 2 C milk, 1 C heavy cream and heat, but don't let it boil. Stir in the rest of the tomato juice and tabasco to taste. Cool and chill. Float slices of cucumber on top when serving.

CHILLED BROCCOLI SOUP

Saute 1 small clove minced garlic and 1/2 C chopped onion in butter, add 2 C boiling hot chicken broth, 1 10-oz frozen package chopped broccoli (or fresh), and cook 10 mins on low. Cover to cool. Add 1/4 t curry powder, 1-1/2 t salt, 1/2 t pepper, and puree in blender for 20 seconds. Stir in 1/2 C half-and-half and chill in covered container. Serve garnished with lemon slices. Serves 6.

FEEDING THE GANG

Summertime means family outings over long weekends, or for even longer periods of time, and this takes a bit of planning. No one wants to be stuck in the kitchen, so the following suggestions might save you time and trouble and start you out on a "game plan" for three days.

When planning the commissary department of your vacation, it's best to be ready for any and all emergencies. Stock your travelling larder with cans of cream of mushroom and chicken soups that can be used for cream sauce bases. Canned corned beef and corned beef hash can be the basis of a filling meal, and Vienna sausages are good either for breakfast or lunch. Canned crab, tuna, and salmon are handy for either salads or sandwiches. Be sure and include pancake and muffin mixes, crackers that are packed in separate packages, syrup, jams, and peanut butter.

Stock up on canned fruit juices preferably with the pop top. Packaged mashed potatoes save time and can be used in several combinations such as corned beef for patties. Play safe and include powdered milk, and appease the sweet tooth with packages of instant puddings.

You can never have enough paper plates and napkins!!

Now for ideas for three nights running.

A Roast Leg of Lamb the first night would be a great way to begin a vacation. If served with baked potatoes topped with sour cream and chives, minted peas, and a salad, it just might stretch for three meals.

The second night chop up some leftover meat and add it to a packaged curry sauce and serve over rice with condiments of chopped egg, bacon bits, mango chutney, chopped green onions and fried bananas, string beans or a salad.

The third night chop up left-over meat and combine with any of the packaged pasta and cream sauce mixes. Serve with a coleslaw or tossed vegetable salad, and fresh fruit for dessert.

Everyone loves turkey!

The first night serve a large roasted turkey. After dinner, remove meat and stuffing from the carcass, store separately in Ziploc bags, and reserve meat for sandwiches at lunch and Creamed Turkey with either leftover stuffing or rice for dinner the second night.

Put the turkey carcass and bones on for soup, and let this simmer along with vegetables of your choice all the second day. The third day skim off fat, remove bones, and save any meat. Add this to soup stock along with leftover creamed turkey, onion soup mix, and cream of mushroom soup. The third night have Turkey Soup for dinner with toasty French bread, cheese, and fruit.

Hamburger is your ace in the hole for three meals, and an all-around crowd pleaser. Ground meat, chicken, or turkey will do.

Buy enough ground meat for three ample meals, and do your preparations and cooking in one full swoop!

Make hamburger patties for the first night. Prepare meat loaf or loaves at the same time, and refrigerate for the second night. Then fry ground meat with chopped onions, add any favorite canned, bottled or packaged spaghetti sauce mix, and refrigerate for the third night. Serve over any type of pasta with a huge tossed salad.

Ham is another winner and meal stretcher. There are many options in serving this entree, and you can end up with a delicious Split Pea Soup when only the bone remains!

Serve a "picture book" ham the first night, and either Baked Beans, Sweet Potato Casserole, Sauerkraut, Curried Fruit Casserole and anything from a Tossed Green Salad to a Fruit Salad.

The second night you have options, too. An inviting platter of cold sliced ham, coleslaw, sliced tomatoes, assorted raw vegetables, cheese, pickles, lettuce, buns, rolls, or bread.

Or serve Creamed Ham. Make a rich cream sauce with a spot of sherry and add diced ham and sauteed mushrooms. Pour over cooked broccoli in casserole. Top with crushed cracker crumbs and Parmesan cheese. Serve with rice.

Another option for another night is **Macaroni, Ham and Cheese Casserole**. In a greased casserole layer cooked elbow macaroni, chopped ham, shredded cheddar cheese, and cover with layer of crushed crackers. Repeat layers, then pour milk over all. Bake in 350 oven for 50 mins. (Basic recipe: 2 cups of everything but 2-1/2 cups of milk.)

One night have a filling **Split Pea Soup**. Follow the directions on the split pea package and let this simmer several hours, stirring occasionally. If there isn't too much meat left on the bone for bits in the soup, add sliced Portuguese sausage.

Meaty Soups and Canned Salmon can be appealing.

Prepare a hearty soup at home, refrigerate, remove fat, and heat for the first night. Combine several meaty soup bones and extra lean stew meat, water, beef broth or V-8 Juice, vegetables of your choice, and a hint of minced garlic. Simmer gently for several hours for a rich, thick soup. Serve over rice with a tossed salad for the first night.

For the second night make **Salmon Patties**. De-bone canned salmon, break up, and mix with enough mashed potatoes (boxed or fresh), chopped green or white onions, chopped parsley, and season to taste. Form into patties, dredge in flour to coat well and leave in refrigerator to set. Fry in oil until crispy and brown. Serve with peas and packaged biscuits.

Or if time is of the essence, cream canned salmon, de-boned and flaked, with thawed or drained canned peas and serve over rice.

The third night add more liquid to soup if need be, then add cooked elbow macaroni, sliced Portuguese sausage or chopped hot dogs, and chopped cabbage to soup, and simmer to cook cabbage, about an hr. Check seasoning. Enjoy with Saloon Pilots and reward everyone with a fancy dessert.

Vacations are to relax and enjoy. So start in the kitchen!

NOTES

Ducks   *Courtesy of Louise Yardley*

SEPTEMBER

◆

*It's September! Labor Day falls on the first Monday
of the month and heralds the end of a lazy summer, the return to
normal routine, and the beginning of a new school year.*

It's time for many people to think about packing Box Lunches and brown bags. Sandwiches become very important in the daily diet. Think about experimenting with some new types of Bread to offer everyone a pleasant surprise!

BOX LUNCHES

A well-balanced lunch consists of something hearty, raw, and sweet, a healthy drink, and accent on foods needed for good health. When you're packing a lunch, try to remember that variety is the spice of life and create tempting offerings of various colors, flavors, and textures. Don't wait to enclose an "I love you" only on special days.

Stock up on individual packages of assorted nuts and chips, mustard and catsup, miniature S&P shakers, and canned fruit juices if they don't want the bother of a thermos. Make up individual packages of mixed dry fruits and keep packages of individually wrapped homemade cookies in the freezer. They'll be just right for lunch, and thaw better in the wrapper.

Once in a while surprise them with cold cash wrapped in a note telling them to buy a treat!

Sandwiches are the backbone of most lunches, are easy to prepare, convenient to carry, and require no utensils.

Sandwich making can be a creative art, really, so vary them with different kinds of breads, scones, buns, bagels, pita bread, or raisin bread.

The ready-sliced loaves make sandwiches look neater, and are much more convenient than struggling with a bread knife for uniform slices.

Occasionally you can vary the menu and replace the familiar sandwich with different flavored bread sticks packed with cubes of various cheeses and cold cuts.

Frozen sandwiches really can't compare with the freshly made ones. You can keep a supply of freshly made fillings in covered containers in the refrigerator for daily fresh sandwiches.

When using meat, cold cuts, or cheese, it's better to use several thin slices than one thick slab.

Keep sandwiches securely wrapped in individual bags or wrappings.

Butter or spread the bread slices generously right to the edge.

Keep cakes and cookies for the lunch box simple...no fussy frosted cakes or cream fillings!

Split yesterday's cornbread and fill it with plain crispy bacon, or mix bacon with peanut butter; or fill with chopped Vienna sausages mixed with relish and mayonnaise for spreading consistency.

Add a dash of curry powder to mashed liverwurst and mix well with mayonnaise to spread between slices of rye bread.

Scramble an egg with bits of chopped ham and green onions and shape it to fit between 2 slices of bread. If you butter the slices first, then you can add a thin layer of catsup over the egg for spice.

Add a bit of lemon juice and dill seed to tuna, and chopped white or green onions, if you dare, with enough mayonnaise for spreading consistency.

Peanut butter combines well with: mashed bananas, crumbled, crispy bacon, chutney, jelly, or chopped green or red bell peppers. Spread between buttered slices of any type bread.

Don't put lettuce leaves in the sandwich. Place crisp, dried lettuce leaves in a plastic bag to add to sandwich later or eat as is.

Left-over meat loaf makes excellent sandwiches or place a slice or two in sandwich bag with another bag containing a slice of cold macaroni and cheese.

Chop hard-boiled egg and combine with equal amount of chopped kamaboko, S&P to taste, and mayonnaise for spreading consistency.

If you're trying out something new, include an old favorite for the second choice...just so they have a back-up.

Don't sell a good salad short in the lunch box. Use disposable, no-leak containers such as clean cottage cheese or yogurt cartons.

Combine chopped raw cabbage with chopped apples and toss with a zippy oil and vinegar dressing.

Remove seeds from unpared cucumber, cut in strips, and either salt and pepper them well or soak in Japanese vinegar, drain, and put in sandwich bag.

Combine a package of chopped walnuts and raisins with an apple.

Combine drained canned kidney beans with chopped celery, green peppers, and onions, and flavor with vinegar to taste. Be sure to pack in secure carton.

Small sweet tomatoes are a salad in themselves.

Carrot sticks and stalks of tender celery may become boring, but you can jazz them up by stringing a few pitted ripe olives onto a few strips.

Peel the tough fiber off the stalks of broccoli and either slice or cut in strips, soak in Japanese vinegar, drain, and add to bag.

You can do the same with cauliflowerettes, too.

Include lots of fresh fruits and vegetables that are in season.

Soak hard-boiled eggs in a mixture of half beet juice and vinegar, and they won't become boring.

For a heartier meal, combine leftover mashed potatoes with either salmon or tuna, chopped parsley, and onions and fry in butter to brown and crispen. Wrap well in tin foil and send along with a mini package of catsup.

Fill the thermos with a variety of cold juices for warm days and piping hot soups when it's cold. You can add crackers for the latter.

CORNED BEEF BUNWICHES

Split 8 to 10 hamburger buns, remove soft center, and butter lightly. Combine 1 12-ounce can corned beef, shredded, 1 C shredded sharp cheese, 1/2 C chopped stuffed green olives, 1/2 C chili sauce, 2 T Worcestershire sauce, 1 T mustard, and optional one chopped round or green onions. Fill buns, wrap each bun separately in foil, and heat in 375 oven for 25 mins or until heated through.

SALAMI

You can easily make your own Salami.

Combine and mix well: 8 cloves minced garlic, 2 lbs extra lean ground beef, 1 T ea Hungarian paprika, salt, coarsely ground black pepper, onion powder, dill seed, Liquid Smoke, and 1 t ea basil, whole coriander seed, whole pickling spice, and mustard seed.

Shape into 2 logs, each about 10 in long. Cover and refrigerate over-night. Uncover, place on broiling rack of pan and bake in 225 oven for 2 hrs. Cool and coat generously with additional paprika before slicing.

Dip leftover sandwiches in a batter of beaten eggs, a dash of baking powder, and a bit of milk. Fry in half oil and butter until each side is crispy and brown. Soggy tuna sandwiches are especially good.

Add chopped and drained chutney to your grilled cheese sandwich, and broil the cheese side first to melt, then turn to toast chutney side.

BREADS

HOPE CLARKE'S PUMPKIN APPLESAUCE BREAD

Cream 1/3 C butter with 1-1/3 C sugar, add 2 eggs, and 1/2 C ea applesauce and mashed pumpkin. Combine and fold in 1-3/4 C flour, 1 t ea baking soda and salt, 1/4 t baking powder, 1/2 t ea cinnamon and nutmeg, and add 1/2 C apple juice gradually. Fold in 1/2 C raisins and 1 C chopped walnuts. Turn into greased loaf pan, bake 1 hr at 350 or until pick inserted in middle comes out clean.

BILL ATKINS' PRUNE BANANA NUT BREAD

Combine 1-3/4 C flour, 1/2 t ea salt and baking soda, and 2 t baking powder in a bowl. Beat 2 eggs until frothy. Mash 1 C bananas. Chop and flour 1/2 C ea prunes and macadamia nuts.

In another bowl combine 3/4 C sugar, 1/2 C oil, and eggs. Add the prunes, nuts and bananas. Blend thoroughly.

Fold into flour mixture until well blended. Pour into greased bread pan and bake at 325 for 1 hr or until brown and toothpick tests for doneness. Remove from oven and allow to stand 10 mins before removing from pan.

SYBIL DEAN'S BANANA BREAD

Place following ingredients in bowl and stir well: 1 C vegetable oil, 4 t baking soda, 2 C sugar, 4 eggs, 2-1/2 C ripe, mashed bananas, 2-1/2 C flour, 1 t salt, 1 C ea mincemeat and chopped nut meats.

This makes 3 large loaves. Bake in 350 oven for 1 hr. Or for 4 small loaves, bake in 350 oven for 45 mins. Best to grease pans and line with wax paper. It's the mincemeat that makes the subtle difference!

APRICOT AND BANANA BREAD

Combine 1 C mashed, ripe bananas and 1/4 C buttermilk.

Sift 1-1/4 C flour with 1 t baking powder and 1/2 t ea salt and baking soda.

Cream 1/3 C shortening with 2/3 C sugar, add 2 eggs, and beat thoroughly. Add banana mixture alternately with flour and mix just until blended.

Stir in 1 C whole bran, 3/4 C chopped dried apricots, and 1/2 C coarsely chopped walnut meats. Turn into a greased 9x5 in loaf pan and bake in 350 oven for 45 min or until pick inserted comes out clean.

APRICOT NUT BREAD

Soak 1/2 C dried apricots, diced, in 1 C water for 30 mins and drain.

Blend 1 C sugar with 1 well beaten egg and add 2 T melted butter. Blend in 2 C flour sifted with 1 T baking powder, 1/4 t baking soda, and 3/4 t salt alternately with 1/2 C orange juice combined with 1/4 C water. Add 1 C sliced almonds and apricots and blend well. Bake in greased loaf pan 1-1/2 hrs in 350 oven.

CRANBERRY FRUIT NUT BREAD

Preheat oven to 350. In a bowl mix together: 2 C flour, 1 C sugar, 1-1/2 t baking powder, 1 t salt, and 1/2 t baking soda.

Stir in 3/4 C orange juice, 1 T grated orange peel, 2 T shortening, and 1 well beaten egg. Mix until well blended.

Stir in 1 C fresh or frozen cranberries, coarsely chopped, and 1/2 C chopped nuts. Turn into 9x5 in loaf pan, greased on bottom only. Bake 55 - 60 mins until toothpick inserted in center comes out clean. Cool thoroughly before serving.

RAISIN NUT BREAD

Combine 2 t baking soda with 2 C boiling water and pour over 2 C raisins. Let stand until cool.

Cream 2 T shortening with 1-1/2 C light brown sugar until fluffy. Add 1/2 t salt and 2 well beaten eggs. Mix well and add raisins and 3 C flour mixed with 1 t baking powder. Fold in 1 C chopped walnuts. Bake in greased loaf pans in 350 oven for 1 hr.

LAVASH

Mix 2-3/4 C flour, 1/4 C (or less if you don't want it sweet) sugar, 1/2 t ea salt and baking soda, and 1 T ea sesame and poppy seeds. Cut in a block of softened butter until it is the consistency of tiny peas. Then mix in 1 C buttermilk.

Mix well, then divide in 3 portions. Cover a large surface with flour and roll out dough a little at a time so you can roll it out as thin as possible. This is the secret of good lavash! Keep flouring, turning, and then lift it onto ungreased cookie sheets and bake in 350 oven, but keep watching as it browns quickly...about 12 mins. Remove to cool on rack and when cold, break up into smaller pieces and store in tightly covered jars.

ZWIEBACK

Beat 3 eggs with 1/2 C sugar until very thick. Add 1-1/2 C flour, and 2 T baking powder, and 1 t anise flavoring. Mix carefully, put in well greased loaf pan, and bake 45 mins in 350 oven. When it is cold, cut in 1 in slices and return to the oven to dry out slowly. Makes 12 slices.

WHOLE WHEAT BANANA BREAD

Combine 2 C whole wheat flour, 1 T wheat germ, 1 t baking soda, and 1/2 t salt in large bowl. Combine 2 eggs, 2 C cut-up ripe bananas, 1/2 C honey, 1/4 C vegetable oil, 1 T lemon juice, and 1/2 t vanilla in blender container and puree until well blended. Blend with flour mixture, add 1/2 C chopped walnuts, and stir with rubber spatula until well blended. Pour into greased 8x5x3 in loaf pan and bake at 350 for 45-55 mins or until pick comes out clean. Cool on rack before removing. Freezes well.

WHOLE WHEAT BREAD

Combine well: 2 C whole wheat flour, 2 T sugar or less, 1/2 t salt, 2 t baking soda, 1 t baking powder, and set aside.

Combine 1 C sour milk (add 1 t vinegar to fresh milk) and 2 T molasses. Pour into dry mixture and blend together. Pour into buttered loaf pan and bake in 350 oven for 40 mins.

ELOISE WINSTEDT'S CORNBREAD WITH CRANBERRY

Prepare 1 package corn muffin mix (8-oz), adding milk and egg as directed. Stir in 1 C chopped cranberries and 1/2 C chopped walnuts. Pour into greased 8-in square pan and bake in 350 oven for 25 min or until inserted pick comes out clean. Serve warm with butter or as is. Serves 6.

This tastes wonderful and looks beautiful with the bits of red that look like cherries...but tastes better.

CHIYANO TAKEMOTO'S PUMPKIN BREAD

Combine 1 C oil, 2 C pureed pumpkin, 4 slightly beaten eggs, and 2/3 C water.

Sift together 2-1/2 C flour, 2 t baking soda, 1 t salt, 3 t cinnamon, 1 t nutmeg, and 3 C sugar and fold into first mixture. Add 1 C ea chopped nuts and raisins. Bake in 2 loaf pans at 350 for 1-1/2 hrs.

QUICK CHEESE BREAD

Combine 2 C flour, 1-1/2 t baking powder, 1/2 t baking soda, 1 t salt, 2 t dry mustard, and 1 C shredded sharp cheese. Set aside.

Beat 2 eggs, 1 C buttermilk, and 1/4 C oil with beater and add all at once to flour mixture. Mix until just moist. Pour into greased 9x5x3 in pan and bake in 375 oven for 45-50 mins or until pick inserted comes out clean. Cool 10 mins and invert on rack. This is delicious toasted.

DARK WALNUT BREAD

Stir 1 C unsifted whole wheat flour into 1-1/4 C flour, 2-1/2 t baking powder, 1 t baking soda, and 3/4 t salt. Sift together and stir in 1/2 C packed brown sugar. Add 1-1/2 C sour milk or buttermilk, 2 T oil, and stir until smooth. Add 3/4 C chopped walnuts. Pour into well-greased 9x5x3 in loaf pan. Decorate with walnut halves and sections of oranges, sprinkle with brown sugar, and bake 1 hr and 20 min in 350 oven or until done.

SCONES

Sift together: 2 C flour, 3 t baking powder, 1 t salt, 1-1/2 T sugar, and make a well. Mix and add 1/3 C milk, 2 beaten eggs, and 3 T melted oleo. Mix lightly, pat or roll 1/4 in thick, and cut in triangles. Brush with milk or egg diluted with water, sprinkle with sugar, and bake on a greased pan in 375 oven about 15 mins.

SPOON BREAD

This is a versatile dish that can either be eaten as is, with syrup, or as a starch with the entree...but not in a sandwich!

Pour 1 C boiling water over 3/4 C corn meal, 3 T butter, and 1 t salt. Cool to lukewarm, then add 1 C milk, 3 well-beaten eggs, and 2 t baking powder. Pour into well-buttered casserole and bake 40-60 mins in 350 oven until set.

SOUR SODA BREAD

Combine 2 C whole wheat flour, 2 C flour, 1 t baking powder, 1-1/2 t baking soda, 2 T sugar, and dash of salt in a large bowl. Add 1 pt plain yogurt or buttermilk and mix and knead until soft dough forms. It should feel wet. Turn onto lightly floured surface and knead a few times, just till dough sticks together, and then form into a round loaf. With a floured knife, make a few slits on top and place on lightly greased baking sheet.

Bake in 375-400 oven for about 20-30 mins or until bread is golden brown and the insides are cooked. Serve immediately with butter.

ZUCCHINI NUT BREAD

In a large bowl sift together: 2 C flour, 1 t cinnamon, 1/2 t ea baking soda and salt, 1/4 t baking powder, and set aside.

In another large bowl, beat 2 eggs until foamy. Gradually add 1-1/3 C sugar, 2/3 C oil, and mix well after each addition. Beat in 2 t vanilla.

In blender at low speed, beat dry ingredients into egg mixture until well blended. Stir in 1-1/3 C shredded zucchini and 1/2 C chopped pecans with a rubber spatula or spoon. Pour batter into greased 9x5 in loaf pan and bake in 350 oven for 1 hr and 15 mins or until pick inserted in center comes out clean. Cool in pan 10 mins. Remove, cool completely on rack, and sprinkle with confectioner's sugar if desired.

Autumn Leaves   *Courtesy of Mrs Donald Woodrum*

OCTOBER

◆

It's October!
Fall is in the air!

On the 16th we remember the romantic Princess Kaiulani's birthday. Tea Time is a cozy hour to gather a few friends together to catch up and chat over a refreshing cup of tea. Or maybe you'll want to gather a few friends for Cocktails before the holiday rush. Don't forget the goblins on the 31st!!!

TEA TIME

In Kaiulani's day, tea was served under the banyan tree at Ainahau in Waikiki and welcomed as a lovely break between the afternoon and evening activities.

Tea time is still a time to relax in the afternoon, have a social hour with friends over a spot of tea, or gather friends together for a special occasion. Tea can be the simplest fare of the day or a lavish high tea with all sorts of heavier foods.

Basic fare with tea is thin sliced buttered bread or toast with jam. On a cool day it's nice to have hot buttered biscuits, scones, English muffins or crumpets with jam, or just cinnamon toast. It becomes a party when sliced pound cake or rich cookies are added.

High tea is almost a meal in itself. You might offer a big platter of crackers or slices of apple with a variety of cheeses and jam, fresh fruit and cream, stuffed eggs and celery, and hearty, meaty sandwiches.

A tea party needn't be a bother and a chore, and you certainly don't need elaborate silver pots and delicate china to entertain. You will, however, need a sizeable table as the focus point of your party. Besides the spoons and tea napkins, have a large tray to hold a pot of the brew, a pot for hot water to dilute tea if too strong, a small pitcher of milk (never cream), a bowl of sugar, a dish of sliced lemon, speared with cloves if you wish, and a receptacle that was referred to in the olden days as the "slop dish"...and it was just that! It held the dregs of lemon, etc. so as to re-fill a fresh cup of tea. It's nice to have a bowl of fresh mint sprigs for color and flavor, and a flacon of rum tops it all off.

Around this place cups and either saucers or larger plates to hold the food. Have several plates of sandwiches, a cake platter of petit fours or lady fingers, lacy cookies, and mints or chocolate bon bons. Try not to make things tricky and difficult to bite into and eat! One has to be lady-like at a Tea Party.!

Little children love tea parties, too, and this calls for patience, steady nerves, and preferably a spot outdoors. It's an exciting event and they love to dress up and play grown-ups, but tea for the young should be weak...more milk than tea...and warm. Give them a choice between cambric tea or cold juice garnished with slices of fruit or cherries.

For a Children's Tea Party, sandwiches made of chopped nuts mixed with just enough thick honey and softened butter to make a crunchy consistency might tempt them instead of the usual peanut butter.

To them a tea party means extra special goodies, but keep in mind that even though it's a party, you don't want to send them home sick! Think about lightly frosted mini muffins and oatmeal or fruity, nutritious cookies besides dishes of jelly beans and sliced fruit.

LIQUID REFRESHMENTS

The rule of thumb for a well-brewed pot of tea is 1 t of tea leaves per person, and then add 1 for the pot. Pour boiling water over the leaves and allow 3-5 mins for tea to steep, then stir slightly so that the strength of the tea is uniform.

It's perfectly acceptable to add a half-pot of hot water to the tea grounds after you've poured the first round. It takes away the bitterness for the second cup.

To make a plain **ICED TEA** with a full-bodied tea flavor, put 4 T of tea leaves in a quart jar and fill with cold water. Set the jar in full sunlight for 2 hrs. If there is no sun, let tea stand for 12 hrs at room temperature. Strain and add sugar, lemon juice, and crushed mint to taste, and serve over crushed ice in tall glasses with a sprig of mint.

MRS. RICHARD COOKE'S ICED TEA

Make a syrup of 2 C sugar and 1 pt water. Pour 2-1/2 qts boiling water over 1/2 C tea leaves, and steep for 3 mins. Strain, add syrup and 4 sprigs of fresh mint. After it cools, add juice of 5 lemons. Serve icy cold with sprigs of mint.

ROSA BULNES' ICED TEA

In a pitcher put 5 T ice tea mix, 5 glasses of water, 2 T pineapple juice, some mint leaves and 1 C of ice. Mix well and serve.

TEA PUNCH

To 3 C of strong green tea add the rind of 6 lemons. Stir together, then drain and add a C of good rum and serve over cracked ice.

ICED COFFEE

To prepare a good glass of iced coffee, start with a strong brew and sweeten to taste when still hot. Cool in covered jar in refrigerator. Serve over ice cubes, and for a special touch add a dash of rum, chocolate, or honey. With a scoop of coffee or vanilla ice cream, it can be passed as a dessert!

COFFEE PUNCH

Whip a pt of cream, gradually add 3/4 C sugar, and add 1/4 C rum drop by drop. Add 1 qt strong cold coffee, beat thoroughly, pour into pitcher to keep cold, and serve.

TEA SANDWICHES

The rule of thumb for tea sandwiches is that they be made on the thinnest fresh bread possible, filled with a delicious variety of fillings, de-crusted, and cut into quarters.

Tea time is no time to have fillings heavy on onions or strong spices. Keep it light and delicate.

You may prepare the fillings in the morning, make up your sandwiches and wrap two or three together in wax paper securely, and cover with a damp linen tea towel. Refrigerate the sandwiches until the afternoon just before you're ready to serve them. Arrange sandwiches attractively on sandwich plates around a sprig of dry parsley or watercress, and cover completely with Saran Wrap.

Soften cream cheese and add finely chopped preserved ginger with just enough syrup to moisten to spreading consistency. Especially delicious with buttered date-nut bread.

Add equal amounts of finely chopped watercress to softened cream cheese, a few drops of lemon juice, Worcestershire sauce, S&P to taste, and enough mayonnaise for proper spreading consistency.

Combine equal portions of mashed avocado and softened cream cheese, a few drops of lemon juice, tabasco, S&P to taste, and blend well with enough mayonnaise or yogurt for spreading consistency, if needed.

It makes for a smoother filling if you grate hard-boiled eggs instead of mashing them with a fork. Add mayonnaise for spreading consistency and season to taste with hint of curry powder, onion salt, and pepper. You may even add softened cream cheese for a richer filling. Or add chopped kamaboko to plain mashed eggs and mayonnaise.

CUCUMBER SANDWICHES

Soak thinly sliced cucumbers in salted water for 1/2 hr, drain, rinse well, and pat dry between cloth. Place between buttered slices of whole wheat bread, and just moisten with mayonnaise.

CHICKEN SANDWICH

Finely mince cooked chicken, celery, and parsley and combine with mayonnaise. Or add to this: finely chopped chutney with some of the syrup, dash of curry powder, and S&P to taste.

FRANCIE HAINES' MUSHROOM AND MINT SANDWICH

Cut 4 or 5 large mushrooms in thin slices and cook quickly in a little butter with S&P to taste. Add heaping t of chopped mint, cool, and serve between buttered brown bread.

TOMATO SANDWICHES

Cut firm tomatoes in half with sharp knife before slicing them very thin. Sprinkle slices with sweet basil mixed with S&P and a whisper of sugar. Lay them on thin slices of white bread that have been buttered or spread with mayonnaise.

TONGUE SANDWICHES

Lay slices of thinly sliced tongue on buttered bread and spread thinly with mild mustard and creamy horseradish.

MISCELLANEOUS

Remove crusts from 8 1-in thick slices of white bread and cut into 1-in strips. Combine 2 T ea butter and honey and 1 C corn syrup and cook slowly until butter melts.

Mix 1-1/2 C crushed corn flakes, 1/2 C finely chopped nuts, and 1 t grated lemon rind. Dip bread sticks in warm syrup, roll in crumbs, and bake in 425 oven for 10 mins or until golden brown.

HOT CINNAMON TOAST

Cut slices of white bread 1/2 in thick, remove crusts, slice into sticks 1/2-in wide and brush generously with melted butter. Roll in mixture of cinnamon and sugar, coating all sides very well. Put under broiler to toast each side.

HOT ROLLED SANDWICHES

Remove crusts from thinnest slices of white bread and spread with softened butter then any type of jelly or marmalade. Roll slices in waxed paper for a firm shape and refrigerate. Before serving, brush with melted butter and toast under broiler, turning so all sides are browned and toasted.

For an intimate "cup of tea", butter very thin slices of white bread, sprinkle a mixture of sugar and cinnamon over the butter, and top with another buttered slice of bread. Cut in half or quarters and place in heated waffle iron to brown. Serve hot.

Slice a pound cake into finger strips, brush with melted butter, and roll in a mixture of cinnamon and sugar.

Bake in 350 oven for 10 mins. Seal securely until time to serve.

Cube slices of fresh fruit in season and thread on bamboo sticks.

PUPUS

Today it's accent on food at cocktail parties, and guests love to gather around a table groaning with hot and cold pupus attractively arranged.

It's a hospitable and thoughtful hostess who offers a bowl of heavy soup or chowder when it comes to "one for the road."

One of the most popular pupus, especially for men, is the platter of assorted small sandwiches. Make them up with fillings of chicken, meat, cheese, and egg, but be prepared to make a large quantity.

A platter of raw vegetables with a not-too-fattening dip is always welcome, especially to the dieter.

If you use salami for any reason, be sure and skin it first before slicing paper thin.

CRISPY CRACKERS

Crispy Crackers are so good they disappear like magic!

Submerge and soak soda crackers (saltines) in a pan of ice water for 1/2 hr. Remove ever so gently with slotted pancake turner, pat dry on paper towel, and place on well-buttered cookie sheet. Spread generously with melted butter and bake in 325 oven for 50-60 mins.

CAVIAR AND EGG PUPU

Caviar and Egg Pupu is eye-catching and delicious.

Mash 4 hard-boiled eggs while hot, add dollop of butter, and spread over bottom of pretty, flat serving dish. Add finely chopped onions to carton of thick sour cream and layer on top. Spread red and black caviar in a wedge design over cream, with sprigs of parsley in the middle. Chill well and serve with crackers or thin slices of buttered, crisp toast rounds.

JANE NAKASHIMA'S POT STICKERS

Jane Nakashima's Pot Stickers are a hearty offering.

Squeeze and drain 3/4 lb finely chopped won bok and combine with 1/2 lb ground pork, 2 t cornstarch or 1 egg, 1 T ea sesame oil, sherry, and soy, 1/2 t salt, 1/4 t sugar, and 1/2 C chopped green onions.

Place 1 T of filling in center of won ton wrapper, dampen edges slightly, fold in half, and seal.

Heat 2 T salad oil in skillet, arrange dumplings in skillet, and cook over medium heat till bottoms are brown. Pour in 1/2 C water, cook covered on low heat for 10 mins or until water evaporates. Repeat until all dumplings are cooked. Serve hot with soy and mustard sauce. Makes 3 doz.

HOT LOBSTER DIP

Whip 1 C mayonnaise together with 1 8-oz package softened cream cheese and dash of garlic powder. Mix well. Rinse 1 12-oz can lobster or crab meat, break into small chunks, and pat dry. Fold into mayonnaise mix and spread thinly in buttered 7x10 in. Pyrex pan, sprinkle with slivered almonds, and bake 30 mins in 350 oven. Serve hot surrounded by crisp crackers or large Fritos.

POOR MAN'S PATE

Mix thoroughly 1 8-oz package softened cream cheese and 1/2 lb braunschweiger. Add 1 T mayonnaise, 2 T chopped chives, heaping t of mustard, 1 T Worcestershire sauce, and 1/2 jigger of bourbon. Mix well and serve with cocktail rye rounds or crackers.

CHEESE MUFFINS

These are handy to have all prepared in the freezer just ready for heating. They are also excellent with soup or salad.

Butter English muffins and top generously with grated sharp cheese mixed with minced garlic or onion to taste. Broil in oven until cheese melts and browns lightly.

To Freeze: put muffins on cookie sheet, freeze, and return to freezer in Ziploc bag.

VARIATIONS ON FILLING WHITES OF EGGS FOR PUPUS

Carefully remove yolks of hard-boiled eggs from whites and mash.

Add mayonnaise and anchovy paste to blend.

Use equal amounts of grated Parmesan cheese, chopped parsley, and enough white wine to moisten properly.

Add equal quantities of shredded crab or shrimp. Moisten with lemon juice, mayonnaise, chopped parsley, and S&P to taste.

Add double amount of bacon bits to mashed yolks, dash of mustard, mayonnaise to hold it together, and S&P and Worcestershire sauce to taste.

Add curry powder and S&P to taste, mayonnaise to blend, and fill whites. Sprinkle with finely chopped peanuts.

CURRIED PECANS

Combine 1/4 C olive oil, 1 T curry powder, 1 T Worcestershire sauce and 1/8 t cayenne pepper in skillet over moderately high heat until well blended. Add 2 C pecan halves and stir until well coated.

Line a cookie sheet with brown paper and spread nuts evenly over pan. Bake 10 mins in 300 oven, check frequently, and mix. Cool and store in air-tight container.

TOM'S POTATO PUPU

Boil the smallest new potatoes you can find until tender, cut in half, remove flesh, and mash. Add cream cheese, grated garlic and onion, chopped chives, and S&P to taste. Refill skins and refrigerate. Top with sprigs of parsley when serving.

MUSHROOM PUPU

Saute chopped mushrooms and onions (as needed) in butter. Add minced cooked chicken and chunks of softened cream cheese, and stir until cheese is melted. Toast one side of slice of French bread and spread mixture on untoasted side. Broil until browned and bubbly and serve hot.

CHEESE PUPU

Lace cheddar cheese soup with sherry and heat well. Pour into chafing dish and keep warm to serve with toasted bread sticks for dunking.

QUICK PUPU

Cover a small package of cream cheese with a dash of lemon juice, finely minced onion, shredded crab, and chili sauce. Garnish with parsley and serve with crackers.

CREAMY AVOCADO DIP

Peel, remove seed, and mash 1 ripe avocado. Blend with juice of 1 lemon, 1 t garlic salt, 1 C sour cream, 1/3 C chopped fresh dill, and S&P and tabasco to taste. Serve with corn chips.

FANCY STEAK TARTARE

Mix 1 lb lean ground sirloin or chuck with 1/2 small jar drained capers, 1/2 tube anchovy paste, 1/2 T fresh ground pepper, 1 raw egg, and garlic salt. Combine thoroughly with hands and form into mounded ball. Cover, chill, uncover and serve with party rye or Rye Crisp. Garnish with parsley or capers.

For extra zing, add tabasco sauce to taste.

PORK PUPU

Roast 1 6-lb pork butt in 350 oven 3-4 hrs until thoroughly cooked and fat is cooked off. Cool and slice meat on the diagonal into serving pieces. Set aside.

Simmer for 15 mins: 2 C ea cider vinegar and water, 4 cloves mashed garlic, tabasco and crushed black pepper to taste, 1 chopped onion, 1 t salt, 1/2 t thyme, and 1/2 bottle Liquid Smoke.

Combine sauce and meat in large pan and simmer in 250 oven for 1 hr. Serve in small buns or on party rye.

You may also serve this with cubes of cooked taro or taro cakes.

MARINATED OLIVES

Drain and dry a #300 large can of pitted black olives. Add 1/3 C chopped parsley and 2 cloves garlic, mashed. Barely cover with olive oil, add lemon juice to taste, dash of salt, and marinate a day or two in refrigerator.

CURRIED OLIVE PUPU

Mix 1 4-1/2-oz can chopped ripe olives, 1/4 C diced green onions, 1/3 C grated cheddar cheese, 4 T mayonnaise, pinch of salt, and curry powder to taste. Mix well, spread on untoasted side of French bread slices, and broil till bubbly. Sprinkle finely chopped parsley on top before serving.

PICKLED MUSHROOMS

Drain a 12-oz can of mushroom crowns, save broth, cut them in half, and turn into bowl.

In small saucepan combine 1/2 C mushroom broth with 1/2 C ea tarragon vinegar, and brown sugar, 1/4 t salt, 1/4 t whole black peppers, 1 bay leaf, and 1 clove garlic, sliced. Bring to a boil then pour over mushrooms to cover. Cover bowl tightly and refrigerate for 24 hrs.

Serve with toothpicks.

HUMMUS

Soak 2 C garbanzo peas overnight, drain, and simmer 1-1/2 hrs. Drain. In food processor combine peas with 1-2 garlic cloves, minced, 2 T Tahini Sesame Butter, 1/2 t olive oil, juice of 1 lemon, 3 t soy, 1/2 C water, 1/2 t white pepper, and puree until very smooth.

Use as dip for crackers or raw vegetables.

IRENE NOZAKI'S PORK PUPUS

These can be prepared ahead of time and frozen, then brought out, thawed, and warmed in sauce for the party.

Remove fat from pork butt and cut into 1x1 in squares. Wash with hot water and drain well. Put in bowl and S&P well. Mix enough cream with 1 egg and pour over meat just to dampen. Sprinkle with flour to coat and deep fry. Brown well, cook through, and drain.

Sauce: combine to taste: water, vinegar, and brown sugar, simmer 5 mins, then add the meat and simmer for 1/2 hr or till tender.

Irene never throws out pickle juice, but uses in sauces instead of vinegar.

At a recent 6-8 p.m. cocktail party, the hostess loved to cook and the dining room table served as a veritable display center for her culinary accomplishments.

Available on the buffet were chopsticks, large paper napkins, and ample size plates so that you could help yourself to the tempting array of food and also balance a glass. At one end of the table was an attractive dish of white and red sashimi with a "just right" sauce, not too hot! Next to this was a large round loaf of French bread that had been hollowed out, filled with the most delectable chicken sandwich filling, and covered with the crusty top cut in bit size pieces with which to scoop up the filling. Between this and a large platter of thinly-sliced tender steak was a platter of two kinds of Brie surrounded by lychees stuffed with cream cheese, and red and yellow peppers hollowed out and holding various vegetable sticks with a dip.

At the head of the table was a "picture book" ham, thinly sliced, and ready to enjoy between whole wheat crusty buns buttered or spread with mayo and mustard as you wished. The split salmon was surrounded by bowls of lemon wedges, mayonnaise, capers, and cocktail rye slices.

Additional platters of crispy bacon wrapped around water chestnuts and broiled and shrimp and onion mixes on toasted rounds were passed.

As a piece de resistance, a platter of beautiful chocolate-coated strawberries was presented.

This would come under the heading of "heavy pupus" or a "stand-up buffet"! However, it spells disaster to the dieter!

MISCELLANEOUS

If you are planning a large cocktail party, remember the law of averages works out to 20% no-shows.

Actually, men don't mind making drinks for themselves and others, too, so it's more practical to have help in the kitchen than hire a bartender...unless, of course, it's a large affair.

If you use your own glasses or a supply of inexpensive ones for such occasions, the ratio is 20 glasses per 14 people.

Your guests will appreciate your supplying the best quality paper cocktail napkins.

It is far better to be left with ice the next day than to run out during the party! Don't skimp on ice!

The well-stocked bar should be ready to supply rum, vodka, gin, bourbon, scotch, sherry, bitters, white vermouth, and LOTS OF WINE. Today more people are drinking white wine with an occasional call for red. So have it well chilled along with beer, diet Cokes, and the regular soft drinks. If you don't have a large enough bucket to fill with ice and libations, fill the laundry tubs or washing machine!

Bar Equipment: cocktail napkins, can openers, wine bottle opener, several jiggers, long stirring spoons, pitcher of water, tea towels, big ice container, slop bowl, slices of lemon or lime, green olives for martinis, cocktail onions for gibsons, and lemon rind and toothpicks.

Leave bowls of nuts for guests to nibble on at the bar or on coffee tables, but keep the pupu dishes filled and replenished whether they're being passed or set out on a table.

Remember, your house isn't undergoing a "white-glove" inspection, so relax and have a good time!

Harvest

Courtesy of Louise Yardley

NOVEMBER

It's November!
Time for the fireplace!

As a rule, the first Tuesday of the month is Election Day. November 11th is a day to remember and honor our Veterans. Thanksgiving falls on the fourth Thursday of the month, so "Let's Talk Turkey." Look for the star-shaped Carambola fruit trees in full bloom.

THANKSGIVING PREPARATIONS

Thanksgiving dinner need not be the burden of all day cooking! Pace yourself. During the month, watch the ads for the best buys in frozen turkeys, fresh or canned cranberries, frozen vegetables, olives, etc.

Plan your menu, then make a master chart with the following headings, leaving lots of room for details. List: Pupus, First Course (fruit cocktail, soup or salad), Main Course (fowl/meat, starch, vegetables), Condiments and Relishes, Desserts, Beverages (Sanka/coffee and wine).

From the ensuing list, check off what ingredients you have on hand and list what you must buy. Double-check your condiment and herb shelf.

When you know exactly how many to expect for dinner, count out required silverware, crystal, china, platters, serving and relish dishes, napkins, and check on the tablecloth. You may even want to buy yardage in fall colors and motifs, and whip up a table cloth to fit your table that will eliminate the worry of stains from the centerpiece and dripping candles.

This should allow you enough time to polish and launder if need be. When you have checked and assembled all the needed equipment, put it to one side and cover with a large beach towel.

Buy a frozen turkey when there is a good buy, or place your order early for a fresh chilled bird. Two or three days before the feast, you may buy all the perishables and start thawing the turkey in the refrigerator.

To bypass the last-minute hassle of gravy-making, bake a few turkey parts several days before Thanksgiving and freeze. Add a little stock to the drippings and make the gravy. Keep refrigerated.

The cranberry sauce or salad molds can be made a few days before Thanksgiving. Remember to order the pies, otherwise bake them Thursday morning.

Tuesday before Thanksgiving, set the table without rushing. Arrange the centerpiece, candles, place cards, and set-up the buffet table.

Wednesday you can actually do most of the cooking and prepare: fruit cup, soup, or clean salad greens (if you're serving a first course), carrot and celery sticks, mashed potatoes, and also any creamed vegetable casseroles, sweet potato dishes, or other vegetables that don't take last-minute cooking.

The stuffing can be made on Wednesday, too. Let it cool completely, and store in Ziploc bag until time to stuff the turkey just before roasting. Remember to remove any leftover stuffing from the cavities after the first meal and store separately. Don't take the risk of any warm stuffing left in the bird turning sour and ruining the left-overs.

Thanksgiving day, stuff and roast the bird, then relax!

TURKEY

The rule of thumb for turkey is 1 lb per serving if it weighs 12 lbs or more. Thaw frozen turkey in the refrigerator according to directions, and remove giblet package as soon as thawed. Either simmer giblets in water to cook, chop up and add to the gravy, or chop raw and add to stuffing.

If you are having a large crowd, there are advantages to roasting 2 10-pounders rather than 1 big 22 lb turkey; you can stuff each bird with a different stuffing, there are more joints, dark and white meat, and everybody's happy.

A cleaned 10-lb turkey serves 12.

Rinse turkey and salt it inside and out. Stuff the turkey lightly (don't pack it in), and put any leftovers in a separate casserole to bake.

Sew the opening with stout thread or close with skewers, rub the whole turkey generously with butter, S&P, and lay it breast side up in the roasting pan.

ROASTING METHOD #1

Put buttered bird in 450 oven, uncovered, for 15-20 mins to sear it and keep in the juices. Then loosely cover with aluminum foil and bake at 350 for 20-25 mins per lb, basting to keep turkey moist.

SLOW OVEN METHOD

Place bird, breast side up, on rack in uncovered pan, brush generously with melted butter, and roast in 300-325 oven, allowing 18-20 mins per lb for a 10-14 lb bird.

Baste frequently with more butter, or cover with butter-drenched cheese cloth then baste frequently.

VARIATION

To the roasting pan add: 1 large chopped onion, 2 stalks chopped celery, leaves and all, 2 chopped carrots, 12 sprigs parsley, 2 bay leaves, and thyme, and pour 2 C boiling chicken broth into pan. Place bird on top. This adds to the essence and moistness of the bird. Strained, the liquid can be used to make rich sauce or gravy.

OPTIONS

Today, thanks to the turkey industry, you don't have to wrestle with a big turkey if you are not planning anything special. There are a variety of different turkey parts to serve a smaller gathering, and you have the initial choice of white or dark meat.

Another option is to roast a small chicken or Cornish game hen.

Stuff and roast Cornish game hens like chickens. Rub breasts and legs with butter or oil and roast in 350 oven, allowing 20 mins per lb per bird. Baste with even portion of melted butter and a rose wine.

If there are only two of you, dress up the hen's legs with fancy pants of ruffled, colored paper, and entwine a lei of cranberries around the two birds.

SAVORY CORNISH GAME HENS

Wash and pat birds dry and sprinkle with S&P. Stuff hens with your favorite stuffing and sew up securely.

Melt a stick of butter slowly in frying pan, add 3 T curry, and stir in 1/4 C white wine and cook until blended. Set aside.

Place game hens in pan, baste with sauce, and roast in 350 oven about an hr or till juices run clear when thickest part is pierced. Keep basting with sauce. Last 20 mins, spread mango chutney over the birds and continue basting and roasting. Serve hot.

APRICOT-GLAZED CORNISH HENS

In small bowl mix 3/4 C apricot preserves with 2 T orange juice, 1 T orange brandy, and rind of 1/2 an orange cut in strips.

Place 2 hens, halved, on rack in roasting pan, sprinkle with salt and paprika and roast in 350 oven 1 - 1-1/4 hrs or until fork-tender. Baste frequently with the apricot mixture during the last 30 mins of baking time.

TURKEY PARTS

FOIL BAKED TURKEY BREAST

Sprinkle bottom side of 2 - 2-1/2 lb turkey breast lightly with salt. Cream 2 T ea margarine, Parmesan cheese, and flour, 1/4 t ea dill weed and basil, and S&P to taste. Spread over the skin part of breast.

Place on sheet of heavy foil, bring edges together up and over meat, and fold over twice. Fold ends twice to seal. Place packet on shallow baking pan, bake in 350 oven for 1-1/2 - 2 hrs. Open foil carefully and pour off juices into a small pot. Thicken slightly with cornstarch mixed with white wine or water, and serve over sliced meat. Makes 4-6 servings.

OVEN BARBECUED TURKEY LEGS

Mix: 1/4 C flour, 1 t salt, 1/2 t chili powder, and 1/4 t pepper and dredge 6 turkey legs in mixture. Brown on all sides in 1/4 C heated cooking oil in large skillet. Place in 13x9x2 in baking pan.

Mix 1/2 C ea bottled barbecue sauce and water with 1 crushed chicken bouillon cube, mix well, and spoon over turkey. Cover with foil and bake in 325 oven for 1 hr, uncover, bake 1 hr longer or until turkey is tender. Baste frequently. Serves 4-6.

HALF BREAST OF TURKEY
WITH MUSHROOMS

Place a 2 - 2-1/4 lb breast of turkey in shallow baking pan. Add 1/2 t ea salt, paprika, and tarragon to 2 T of melted butter, and spoon over turkey. Bake in 450 oven for 10 mins.

Combine 1/2 C dry white wine and 1 C sliced fresh mushrooms or 1 2-oz can mushrooms, undrained, and pour over turkey. Lower heat to 325 and bake 1 hr longer, basting once or twice with pan liquid. Remove from oven, transfer meat to serving plate, and keep warm.

Prepare 1 6-oz package dry stuffing mix as directed, using drainage drippings for part of liquid, and add 3 T melted butter. Serves 2.

TURKEY STEAKS PARMESAN

Drizzle 1 lb turkey breast steaks 3/8 to 1/2 in thick with 1-1/2 t lemon juice. Mix 2 T flour with 1 t salt and 1/8 t pepper. Beat 1 egg with tablespoon of water. Dip steaks in seasoned flour and shake off excess, dip in egg and allow excess to drip off, then roll in 1/2 C ea cornflake crumbs and shredded or grated Parmesan cheese.

Heat 2 T ea butter and oil in large skillet, add steaks, and cook quickly, about 2 mins on each side, just until well browned and cooked through. Serve at once garnished with lemon slices and fresh basil sprigs. Makes 4 servings.

STUFFINGS

POULTRY STUFFING

Saute until tender 3/4 C chopped onion and 1 C chopped celery in 1 C butter, then add 1 C chopped parsley, 1 C or more sliced mushrooms, 1/2 C sliced water chestnuts, and 1 C chopped almonds, pecans or walnuts.

Slowly add 1 lb package of Pepperidge Farm stuffing and mix thoroughly with enough stock or water to hold together...about 1-1/2 cups. Check seasonings and add more sage, poultry seasoning, or S&P if you like. Enough for 12-16 lb turkey.

You may also add the raw giblets of the turkey, chopped, to the onions and celery to cook if you like.

STUFFING WITH SAUSAGE

Fry 1/2 lb chopped bacon or Portuguese sausage, crumbled, and optional on chopped kidneys and liver of the fowl. Add enough oil to fry this with 3 C chopped onions, 1 C chopped celery, 1 bunch chopped parsley, 3 grated carrots, and simmer until cooked. Add enough packaged bread stuffing to mix well and season to taste with S&P, marjoram, poultry dressing, sage, and thyme. Stir to mix the bread and vegetables well, whip in a slightly beaten egg, and stir quickly so as to hold the dressing together. Cool and stuff the bird.

TURKEY STUFFING

Cook 1 package frozen chopped spinach according to directions, drain, and squeeze dry.

Saute 2 C ea chopped celery and onions in 1 cube butter.

In a large bowl combine cooled spinach, celery, and onions, 1 small or medium can pitted olives, chopped, 1 C chopped walnuts, and 2 bags bread cubes with herbs. Mix well with 2 forks and add enough chicken broth just to moisten.

Put any leftover stuffing in casserole, add turkey drippings, cover, and warm to heat through. Enough for a 15 lb turkey.

SOUTHERN STUFFING

Make up 1 package corn bread mix according to directions and crumble Add: 2 slightly beaten eggs, 2 C chopped walnuts, 2 T melted butter, 1 C chopped celery, 1 C chopped onions, 1/2 C cream, and S&P to taste. Mix well. This should be enough to stuff a 13 lb bird.

SWEET POTATO STUFFING

Brown 1 lb ground pork sausage and drain off fat. Saute 1 large chopped onion and 1/2 C ea chopped celery and green pepper in 1/2 lb butter until tender. Combine sausage, vegetables, and 2 lbs sweet potatoes, cooked and chopped, 1 t grated orange peel, and 1/4 C chopped parsley.

Add 1 C chicken broth, 1/2 C orange juice, and 2 beaten eggs. Stir well. Combine with 2 7-oz packages prepared cornbread stuffing mix.

This is enough for a 16-20 lb turkey.

For a side dish, place stuffing in greased casserole and bake in 350 oven for 1 hr.

RICE STUFFING

Cook 3 C rice, cool slightly, fluffing with fork.

Saute 2 medium onions, chopped, and 1-1/2 C chopped celery in 3 T butter till soft (do not brown). Add turkey giblets, cooked and chopped, cook gently 1 min more, and add rice. Add 3/4 t ea poultry seasoning and thyme and 1 T parsley flakes. Mix well.

If desired, add 1 small can chopped mushrooms.

This should be enough to stuff a 15 lb bird.

THANKSGIVING VEGETABLES

CREAMED ONIONS

The canned small onions are so good today that you can use them exclusively or mix with the fresh. Blanch small white onions in hot water to easily remove skins, cut off both ends, and cook until just tender. Combine with a white sauce with lots of grated sharp cheddar cheese, turn into casserole, and sprinkle with more cheese and bread crumbs on top.

Bake in oven long enough to heat through, bubble, and brown slightly on top.

CREAMED CAULIFLOWER

Either cook a whole cauliflower head until tender or break head into pieces and cook. Combine with cream sauce in large casserole and sprinkle generously with grated sharp cheddar cheese over all. Bake in oven long enough to heat through, bubble, and brown slightly on top.

ORANGE GLAZED SWEET POTATOES

Boil sweet potatoes in skins until barely cooked, then peel and cut in thick slices. Butter casserole and layer potatoes, sprinkle salt to taste, and cover with lots or orange marmalade. Dot with pats of butter and bake in 325 oven for 30-40 mins, or until nicely candied and brown.

CASSEROLE OF SWEET POTATOES WITH LIME

Layer rounds of cooked sweet potatoes with paper-thin slices of lime between every few slices. Pour melted butter over and sprinkle generously with brown sugar. Bake in shallow casserole in 350 oven until nicely browned.

CRANBERRY SCALLOPED SWEET POTATOES

Pare and slice 6 medium raw sweet potatoes 1/4 in thick and place in alternate layers with 2 C whole cranberry sauce, 1/2 C brown sugar, and dot with 2 T butter in a large, buttered casserole. Cover and bake at 350 about 1 hr or until potatoes are tender.

CANDIED CARROTS

Cook 2 lbs sliced carrots or young baby whole ones in water to cover until tender crisp. Drain, melt 1-1/2 stick oleo in pan, add cooked carrots, and sprinkle with 1/4 C light brown sugar and a dash of nutmeg. Stir occasionally and cook 5 mins, or until carrots are glazed.

SWEET AND SOUR RED CABBAGE

Slice 1 large head red cabbage fairly thin. In large pot fry 1/2 C chopped bacon and add 1/2 C chopped onions to saute. Add cabbage and 1 C burgundy wine, 1/2 C brown sugar, 1 C applesauce, 1 T salt, and 1 t pepper. Turn into casserole, cover, and cook in 350 oven for 1 - 1-1/2 hrs, stirring occasionally.

FANCY ADDITIONS TO GREEN STRING BEANS

Garnish piping hot beans with butter, blanched almonds, and chopped water chestnuts.

To 2 C cooked beans add 1/2 C sauteed mushrooms, 1/3 C sour cream, and 2 T chopped parsley.

SNOW PEAS WITH SESAME DRESSING

Cook 1 package frozen Chinese peas (or fresh if in season) till tender crisp...1 min after it boils.

Cut 1 head cauliflower into flowerettes (about 2 C) and boil 3 mins until tender crisp. Drain vegetables and add 1 can water chestnuts, sliced. Chill mixture and before serving, toss with dressing.

SESAME SEED DRESSING

In jar with lid combine 1/3 C salad oil, 1 T ea lemon juice, vinegar, sugar, and 1/2 clove garlic, minced, 1/2 t salt, and add 2 T toasted sesame seeds. Shake and chill well, and shake again before pouring over greens. Serve on crispy lettuce leaves.

FANCY PEAS

Cook 1 package frozen peas according to directions, drain well, season to taste, add butter and 2 T minced fresh mint. Stir well and serve hot.

PEAS AS DECORATION

Place plain cooked peas around casserole of Creamed Cauliflower or Creamed Onions, and place sprig of fresh parsley in the middle.

CRANBERRY APPLESAUCE

In large pot combine 1 package fresh cranberries with 4 chopped tart apples and 1/2 C water and bring to boil. Turn down heat and stew, stirring occasionally, until really soft and mushy. Put through ricer and add sugar to taste. Keep refrigerated.

Use as a relish, but this is equally good just plain with yogurt or cream.

FRESH CRANBERRY ORANGE RELISH

Combine the following ingredients in a bowl, stir well, cover, and chill overnight: 2 C fresh cranberries, finely chopped, 1 T grated orange rind, 1 medium orange, peeled, sectioned, seeded, and chopped, 1 medium size green apple, cored and finely chopped, 1/2 C sugar or to taste, 1/4 t ginger and nutmeg. Keep refrigerated.

LOW-CAL PINEAPPLE CRANBERRY SAUCE

Combine 16-oz can crushed unsweetened juice-packed pineapple and 4 C fresh cranberries. Simmer until cranberries pop open. Chill. 16 servings.

CRUNCHY CRANBERRY RELISH

In a large bowl mix together: 2 C fresh cranberries, coarsely chopped, 1 large apple, coarsely chopped, 1 C thinly sliced celery, 1 8-oz can crushed pineapple packed in juice, 1/2 C chopped walnuts, and 1 3-oz package low-cal lemon gelatin dessert. Chill. Makes 2 pts.

CRANBERRY MOLD

Dissolve 1 3-oz package red gelatin in 1 C boiling water, add 3/4 C pineapple juice and 1 8-oz can whole berry cranberry sauce. Chill until slightly thickened. Stir in 1 C diced apples or celery and 1/3 C coarsely chopped nuts. Pour into 4 C mold or individual molds and chill until firm. Makes 3-1/2 cups.

SHERRY CRANBERRY

Dissolve 1 C granulated sugar in 1 C dry sherry over low heat, stirring continually. Add 2 C pierced cranberries and 1/2 C coarsely ground walnuts, and simmer until cranberries are thoroughly cooked but not mushy. Jar and refrigerate.

LEMON CRANBERRY SAUCE

Boil together 5 mins: 1 C water and 2 C sugar and add 1 lb cranberries. Cook 5 mins or until all have popped and become transparent. Remove from heat and add 6 generous tablespoons orange marmalade, stir, and add strained juice from 2 lemons. Bottle and refrigerate.

LEFTOVERS

TURKEY ENCORE CASSEROLE

Cook 1 package 6-oz long grain wild rice according to directions and turn into large buttered casserole. Lay 4 C cubed cooked turkey on top.

Mix together: 1 4-oz can sliced water chestnuts, 1/2 C toasted sliced almonds, 1/3 C ea chopped green pepper and pimento, 1/2 C minced onion, and 1 can ea cream of chicken and mushroom soups. Blend, pour over the cubed turkey, and bake uncovered in 350 oven 45 mins.

CREAMED LEFTOVER TURKEY CASSEROLE

Heat 2 T butter in skillet and saute 1 lb fresh mushrooms. Add 2 C diced cooked turkey and cook until heated. Set aside.

Heat 3 T butter, stir in 3 T flour, and gradually add 2 C chicken broth and 1 C heavy cream. Stir over low heat until thick. Add 3/4 C Parmesan cheese, S&P to taste, and the turkey and mushrooms. Pour into casserole and heat until very hot.

If you like pimento, chop some and add to the mixture.

Bake frozen patty shells and when they are prepared, fill with turkey mixture and serve with garnish of chopped parsley.

POST-HOLIDAY LUNCHEON MUFFINS

Saute 1 small chopped onion or 4 whole stalks green onions with 3/4 C fresh mushrooms in a little oleo until limp. Add to 1 C ea grated Monterey Jack cheese and chopped leftover turkey. Blend with 1/2 C or more mayonnaise and spread on English muffins. Broil until bubbly and cheese is melted.

TURKEY CRISTO

Butter 8 slices French bread, add slice of turkey, slice of Swiss cheese, second turkey slices and top with bread slice. Repeat for 4 sandwiches. Cut each in half diagonally and secure with wooden pics.

Combine 1-1/2 C flour, 1/4 t salt, and 1 T baking powder. Beat 1 egg and 1-1/3 C water together and gradually add to flour mixture. Mix well. Heat about 1 in of oil in skillet turned to 375. Dip each sandwich in batter to coat well and fry in hot oil until golden brown, turning once. Drain, remove wooden picks, sprinkle with powdered sugar, and serve immediately with jelly or marmalade.

TURKEY STRATA

Butter 2 slices of bread, cut in 1/4 in cubes, and set aside. Cut 6 slices in 1 in cubes. Place 1/2 unbuttered cubes in bottom of large casserole.

Combine 3 C cooked, diced turkey, 1/2 C ea chopped onions, green pepper, celery, and mayonnaise, season to taste, and spoon over bread in casserole. Sprinkle remaining unbuttered cubes over meat mixture.

Combine 2 eggs and 1-1/2 C milk and pour over mixture. Cover and chill at least 1 hr or overnight, which is better. Just before baking, spoon can of mushroom soup over top and sprinkle buttered bread cubes over all. Bake in 325 oven for 40 mins. Place 1-1/2 C sharp cheese, shredded, over top for last few mins of baking, and bake until cheese is melted.

## FRUIT	NOTES

CARAMBOLA OR STAR FRUIT

The tree is usually laden with waxy, golden-yellow to orange fruit in November and December, and besides good eating, can be used in table centerpieces featuring fruit.

Though there is not much food value, the ripe, sweet, watery pulp of the fruit is delicious when eaten right from the tree.

It is star-shaped when sliced and makes a great addition to salads, fruit cocktails, or to float on exotic drinks.

Place slices of the sour carambola on a roasting chicken to add new dimensions.

It can be pickled or used for chutney and preserves.

JUICE

Wash carambolas and chop into small pieces to put through ricer. Bottle the juice and refrigerate.

CARAMBOLA FRUIT DRINK

Combine 2 C carambola juice and cold water and sugar to taste. Serve over cracked ice.

The Christmas Party   *Collection of the Artist*

DECEMBER

◆

It's December!!
Christmas is in the air! Be sure you've hidden
the Christmas presents well!

This is the season to be jolly, entertain with formal or informal gatherings full of good cheer, and absolve Scrooge and bless Tiny Tim!

Whether you celebrate quietly or with friends, remember food can make it a very special occasion.

CHRISTMAS SPIRIT

In Hawaii we sing "Mele Kalikimaka", and Santa arrives on a surfboard under blue skies and sunny weather.

But like Christmas all over the world, the season is a time for loving, remembering, and worshipping; it's a time for traditions from years past; for joyous caroling and sharing.

Christmas is nostalgia. Vivid childhood memories: our hopes, our dreams, our favorite ornaments, sleepless Christmas Eves, drying wishbones, tempting smells from the kitchen, and surreptitiously preparing presents for family and friends.

The house abounds in people, excitement, anticipation, aromas, mystery, and beauty like no other time of the year. The kitchen becomes a beehive of activity and Christmas dinner, whether celebrated on the eve or day, is a special feast.

New Year's Eve is champagne, caviar, hoopla, and fireworks!

GIFTS FROM THE KITCHEN

CHRISTMAS COOKIES

Combine 1 C mixed chopped candied fruits and peels and 1/2 C ea chopped raisins and pecans with 1/4 C bourbon. Let stand several hours.

In mixer bowl cream 1/2 C butter with 1/2 C packed brown sugar and 1/4 C honey. Beat in 2 eggs. Mix 2-3/4 C flour, 1 t cinnamon, 1/2 t ea baking soda and nutmeg, 1/4 t baking powder, and add to creamed mixture alternately with 1/4 C sour cream. Stir fruit mixture into batter and drop by teaspoons onto greased cookie sheet. Bake in 350 oven 10-12 mins. Cool on wire rack. Makes 5 dozen.

SUGARLESS COOKIES

Cut 1/2 C ea dried prunes, dates, and raisins and boil 6 mins in 1 C water. Add 1 cube margarine and cool. Add 1 beaten egg and 1-1/2 C flour mixed with 1 t ea soda and cinnamon, 1/4 t each salt and all-spice. Mix well, and add 1 t vanilla, and stir in 1 C walnuts.

Drop by spoonfuls on cookie sheet and bake in 350 oven for 9-12 mins.

SHORTBREAD

Blend together 1/2 lb butter and 1/2 C sugar, creaming well. Add 2 C flour gradually until mixture leaves the sides of the bowl and forms a ball. Press into two 8 or 9-inch round layer pans and prick with a fork all over.

Bake in 350 oven for about 30 mins or until a light golden color. While still hot, mark wedges with a knife. 16 small triangles.

AUNT MARY'S GINGER DROPS

Sift together 3 C flour, 2 t ea baking soda and cinnamon, 1 t ground cloves, 2 T ginger, and set aside. Cream 3/4 C ea butter and shortening with 2 C sugar until fluffy, then add 2 eggs, 1 at a time. When mixed, add 1/2 C molasses and flour mixture and blend thoroughly.

Drop by teaspoonfuls onto ungreased pan. Bake cookies in 375 oven 12-15 mins. Makes 6 dozen.

SPICED BANANA FRUIT CAKE

Sift 3-1/2 C flour with 4 t baking powder, and 1 t salt. Mix together 1/2 t soda, 2 t ea cinnamon and ground ginger, 1 t nutmeg, and 1-1/3 C shortening. Gradually blend in 1-1/3 C sugar. Beat in 4 eggs, 1 at a time, beating after each addition.

Add flour mixture alternately with 2 C mashed bananas. Mix 1 C raisins, 1-1/2 C chopped nuts, and 4 C glazed diced fruit and stir into batter. Turn into 2 well-greased, lightly floured 9x5x3 in pans and bake 2 hrs or until done in 300 oven. Keep a shallow pan of hot water underneath cake throughout the baking period. Store cakes in tightly sealed container.

ELENA ATKINS' OLD FASHIONED FRUIT CAKE

This fruit cake is made of all dried fruit.

Add 5 lbs mixed chopped nuts...pecans, walnuts, almonds, macadamias...with 15 lbs mixed, dried, chopped fruits...prunes, raisins, apricots, peaches, bananas, mango, dates, currants, lemon peel, orange peel, figs, etc.

Add 1/2 C brandy, 20 oz marmalade or blackberry jam, 1 t ea allspice and cloves, 4 t ea nutmeg and salt, and 2-1/2 T cinnamon.

Cream 2 lbs butter with 2 lbs brown sugar, 1 C molasses, and 2 dozen eggs, beaten until foamy. Pour this over fruit mixture, add 2 lbs flour, and mix thoroughly. Dough should be fairly stiff, not runny. A little more flour or a little more brandy may be added, as needed.

Grease pans well, line with either waxed or brown paper, and grease paper well. Fill pans 2/3 full and bake at 275 until cake is firm and a straw comes out clean. It will take 2-3 hrs, depending on size. Turn cakes on racks to cool and remove the paper while still warm. Also while still warm, pour about 1/4 C of brandy very slowly over each cake. When cakes are cold, wrap each one and place in an airtight container.

ELOISE WINSTEDT'S DARK FRUIT CAKE

Cream 1 lb butter and 1 lb brown sugar well, add 1 C ea honey and molasses, 1/4 C brandy, and 10 eggs, 1 at a time, beating well between each addition. Add 1 C flour and 1 lb ea raisins, dates, chopped walnuts, and 2 lbs fruit mix, until fully floured.

Add 1 t ea allspice, mace, nutmeg, baking soda, and salt to 3 C flour and mix well into fruit mixture. Turn into 3 greased loaf pans and bake in 275 oven for 1 hr, lower oven to 250, and bake 1-1/2 hrs longer.

Cover cakes with brandy-soaked cheesecloth and store in covered containers.

SUGARED WALNUTS

Boil 1-1/2 C sugar and 1/2 C water to the soft ball stage, and add 1/2 t vanilla. Pour over 3 C walnuts, mix gently with a fork, and put on waxed paper. Work quickly to separate each nut. Cool, and when cold store in covered container.

STUFFED DATES

Blend 2 C sifted powdered sugar, 2 T butter, and about 2 T orange juice or sherry and stuff into pitted dates. Decorate with orange peel or nuts. Fill apothecary jars, brandy snifters, or pretty containers and wrap in bright Christmas paper and ribbon.

FIG NUT BALL

Combine 2 8-oz packages of softened cream cheese with 8-oz package of cut up calmar figs. Mix well, form into balls, and roll in chopped macadamia nuts. Place on waxed paper in fancy box and refrigerate.

BRANDIED PINEAPPLE

Cut fresh pineapple into thick slices, peel, remove eyes, and core and cut slices into chunks or strips. Measure pineapple and place in a crock or glass jar, add equal amount of sugar and 2 oz of brandy for each cup of fruit. Mix well, cover, and stir every day for 2 weeks. It will be ready to put up in jars or attractive glasses. Cover securely and tie with colorful ribbon.

HOLIDAY LIBATIONS

TRADITIONAL EGGNOG BOWL

Beat 6 egg whites until stiff and add 1/4 C sugar gradually while beating. Beat 6 eggs yolks till light and fluffy, adding 1/2 C sugar while beating. Combine whites and yolks together, add 1 pt whipped cream, and mix. Add 1 pt ea milk and bourbon and 2 T rum. Stir thoroughly, chill, and serve in punch cups with grated nutmeg sprinkled over the top. 15 cups.

CHRISTMAS EGGNOG

Beat 5 egg yolks until very light, add 3/4 C sugar, and continue beating until well blended. Slowly add 1/2 C ea brandy and rum, then mix in 4 C ea milk and cream. Fold in 6 stiffly beaten egg whites, pour into punch bowl, and sprinkle with nutmeg. 25 servings.

Be sure ingredients are very cold and leave in refrigerator until time to serve.

COFFEE EGGNOG PUNCH

In large mixing bowl combine 2 32-oz cartons chilled ready-made eggnog, 1/4 C firmly packed light brown sugar, 2 T dry instant coffee, and 1/4 t cinnamon. Beat on low speed till sugar and coffee are dissolved, and stir in 1/4 C ea coffee liqueur and either bourbon or brandy. Chill. Keep refrigerated until ready to serve.

Just before serving, beat 1 C whipping cream with 1/4 C confectioners' sugar and 1 t vanilla till stiff. Pour chilled eggnog into punch bowl and top with whipped cream.

BREAKFAST COGNACKAFFEE

Beat 6 eggs and grated peel of 1 lemon until light and fluffy, gradually add 1/2 C sugar, and beat until thick. Stir in 3 C cold, strong coffee, slowly add 2/3 C brandy or cognac, and serve in chilled glasses. About 12 4-oz glasses.

CHRISTMAS DINNER

ROAST BEEF

Select a large roast beef with at least 5 ribs or more. Count on 3 to 4 servings per lb. Ask the butcher to remove the chine (back bone) and tie it back on to protect the eye in cooking. Rub roast all over with S&P and place fat side up in roasting pan. Sear in 500 oven for 20 mins, reduce to 325, and cook 18 mins per lb for rare and 20-22 mins per lb for medium...counting searing time.

Remove roast to serving platter and let it sit in warm place at least 10-20 mins before carving.

YORKSHIRE PUDDING

A special treat instead of potatoes.

Batter: Sift 2 C flour and 1 t salt together in large bowl, stir in 2 C milk, and beat with electric beater. Add 4 eggs, 1 at a time, beating very hard after each addition. The batter should resemble heavy cream. Refrigerate covered until time to bake.

Pour drippings from roast pan and enough oil needed to make 1/4 C into large pan, and place in oven to heat. Beat the chilled batter again to form bubbles and pour quickly into hot pan. Bake in 450 oven until pudding rises, about 15 mins, reduce heat to 350, and continue cooking 10-15 mins until it has really risen and turned brown and crisp. Cut in wedges and place around roast.

HORSERADISH SAUCE

Combine 1/2 C prepared hot horseradish sauce with 1 C sour cream.

PORK CROWN RIB ROAST

(8 lbs with about 16 ribs)

Combine 1-1/4 t thyme, 1 t salt, 1/2 t ea garlic salt and pepper and sage. Rub seasoning into roast well, place in shallow roasting pan, bone tip up, and cover ends of bones with strips of foil. Roast in 325 oven 35-40 mins per lb or until inserted thermometer registers 170.

Fill roast cavity with stuffing about 1 hr before end of roasting time.

STUFFING

Melt 1/2 C butter in large skillet over low heat, add 1 small chopped onion, 1 large cored and chopped apple, and 1/2 C chopped celery, and cook over medium heat 5-10 mins, stirring frequently. Add 1 C washed cranberries and cook over low heat 5 mins more.

Combine 1 8-oz package cornbread stuffing mix, 1/2 C orange or lilikoi juice, 2 T water, 1 well beaten egg, 1 T brown sugar, 1/2 t salt, 1/4 t ea sage, thyme and poultry dressing, and add to cranberry mixture. Mix well and stuff into roast cavity. Put any leftover dressing into casserole to bake covered.

When roast is done, place on serving platter and garnish with lots of fresh parsley or watercress and red grapes or cranberries. Put ruffled pants on bones. 8-12 servings.

ELOISE WINDSTEDT'S CHRISTMAS SWEET POTATOES

Cook, peel, and mash 4 lbs Island sweet potatoes, not yams. Add 3 T lemon juice, 1/2 stick softened butter, 2 slightly beaten egg yolks, S&P to taste, and turn into 1-1/2 qt casserole. Brush generously with melted butter and top with thin lemon slices. Bake in 325 oven for 45 mins or until thoroughly heated. Decorate top with a lei of fresh cranberries and sprigs of parsley.

SWEET POTATO-APRICOT CASSEROLE

Cook 6 medium sweet potatoes until soft, drain, and peel. Cook 1 C dried apricots in small amount of water about 10 mins and drain.

Combine sweet potatoes, apricots, and 1/4 C butter and beat until fluffy. Add 2 beaten eggs, 2 t finely shredded orange peel, and 3/4 t salt. Turn into ungreased quart casserole, and bake covered in 325 oven for 1 hr. Serves 8.

HOLIDAY STRING BEAN CASSEROLE

Barely blanche 5 packages French-cut frozen beans, drain, and combine with 4 cans cream of mushroom soup and 2 cans French-fried onions. Season with pepper to taste and pour into party casserole. Top with 1 can of French-fried onions and heat until bubbling. Can be done ahead and serves 12.

FROSTED CAULIFLOWER

Combine 1 small jar baby food green peas with 2 T melted butter and enough cream to make a smooth sauce, but it must not be runny.

Place 1 large, cooked cauliflower head in casserole, pour the pea mixture over to frost evenly, sprinkle buttered crumbs over the top, and broil 3 in from top till lightly browned and heated.

GINGERED CARROTS

Peel 2 lbs carrots, cut in thin slices, and steam till tender.

In large frying pan melt 3/4 block of butter, add 2 T finely grated fresh ginger, and fry briefly. Stir in 2 T honey, S&P to taste, then toss in the carrots just to glaze them...about 2 mins. Serve hot. Serves 8.

JOAN ANDERSEN'S HOLIDAY PEAS AND ONIONS

Combine 1 C milk, 2-1/2 T butter, 1 T lemon juice, 2 chicken bouillon cubes, 1 T white wine, and slowly add 2-1/2 T cornstarch mixed with water to form a paste. Cook over medium heat to thicken. Add 1 C grated Jack cheese, dash of S&P, and Worcestershire sauce.

Add 2 cans drained small onions and pour into casserole. Distribute 2 packages thawed frozen peas around the sides, top with canned button mushrooms, and dot with slivered almonds and butter. Cover and bake in 300 oven 25 mins until heated through.

TOMATOES FILLED WITH SPINACH

Adds a colorful red and green touch.

Thaw 1 10-oz package frozen chopped spinach, drain, and squeeze dry. Cut out centers of 6 medium size firm tomatoes, leaving firm outside wall, sprinkle with salt, and stand them upside-down to drain. Chop tomato centers and drain.

Fry 3 slices bacon until crisp, drain, and crumble. In 2 T of bacon fat saute 1/4 C chopped shallots over low heat, add spinach, well-drained tomato pulp, 1 C sour cream, and season with 1/2 t nutmeg and S&P. Stir well, add 1/3 C grated mozzarella cheese, and stir in bacon. When heated through, fill cavity of tomatoes with mixture. Place in slightly buttered baking pan, top tomatoes with 1/2 C cheese, and heat in 375 oven for 15-20 mins.

You can stuff these tomatoes earlier and broil just at serving.

HOLIDAY DESSERTS

EGGNOG PIE

Prepare and bake your favorite 9 in pie crust.

Mix 1 envelope unflavored gelatin, 1/4 C sugar, and 1/4 t salt. Gradually stir in 1-3/4 C dairy eggnog, 1/4 C rum, warm and stir over low heat until gelatin is dissolved. Chill until mixture mounds when dropped from a spoon.

Fold in 1 C whipped cream flavored with 1/2 t vanilla. Mound into prepared pie crust and chill until set. Garnish with bits of red and green maraschino cherries and very finely chopped nuts.

ENGLISH TRIFLE

Cut 1/2 lb bought pound cake, sponge cake, or yellow cake into chunky pieces, and dip each piece into 1/2 C sherry or cognac. Spread each saturated piece with strawberry or raspberry jam and arrange in bottom of serving bowl. Let this stand about an hr.

SOFT CUSTARD

Heat 2 C milk in top of double boiler, but don't boil. Mix together 1/3 C sugar, dash salt, 1-1/2 T cornstarch, and 2 eggs. Gradually add to hot milk, stirring constantly. Cook until thick as mayonnaise, stirring constantly. Remove from heat and add 1/2 t almond extract. Cool, pour over the layer of cake, and cover with 1 C heavy cream, whipped. Decorate with slivered almonds and candied cherries.

FRUIT CAKE PARFAITS

Toss 2 C chopped-up fruitcake with 3 T dark rum and let stand for 10 mins. Soften 1 qt vanilla ice cream slightly, layer ice cream and fruitcake in 6 parfait glasses, then freeze up to 24 hrs. To serve: let stand at room temperature 10 mins to soften, top with well chilled whipped cream, and decorate with slices of candied fruit.

HAZEL MILNOR'S EASY HOLIDAY DESSERT

Warm enough mincemeat to generously top rich vanilla ice cream in individual dessert bowls.

HOT MINCE PIE WITH RUM SAUCE

Prepare enough of your favorite pie crust for top and bottom of 9 in crust.

Filling: Combine 1-lb 12-oz jar prepared mincemeat with 1 T ea brandy and rum, 1 C ea applesauce and coarsely chopped walnuts. Turn into prepared pie crust and place lattice top over filling. Pinch edge and strips together, then press edge of pastry with damp tines of fork. Beat egg yolk with 1 T water and brush only the lattice top, but not the edges.

Bake 30-35 mins or until crust is nicely browned.

Serve with **HOT BRANDY SAUCE**

Mix 1-1/2 C sugar with 1 t cornstarch, add 1 C water, 1 cinnamon stick, 2 pieces lemon rind, 3 whole cloves, and 1 T lemon juice. Boil until slightly thickened, strain, and add 2 T brandy or rum. Serve hot.

MOTHER FARDEN'S PUMPKIN PIE

Prepare unbaked 9 in pie crust.

Filling: Combine in order given and mix well: 1 C cooked mashed pumpkin, 1/2 C sugar, 2 egg yolks and 1 whole egg, 1-1/2 t cinnamon, 1/2 t ea ground ginger and lemon extract, and 1 C milk. Pour into pie shell. Bake in 400 oven 20 mins, lower heat to 375, and bake until filling is thick or knife comes out clean when inserted in middle of pie. Cover with meringue.

MERINGUE

Beat until frothy: 2 egg whites, 1/8 t salt, 1/4 t cream of tartar, and gradually add 4 T sugar, beating constantly until the meringue is stiff and glossy. Then heap it over pie and spread to edges. Bake in 400 oven 8-10 mins to lightly brown.

HEALTHY VERSION OF PLUM PUDDING

Sift together: 1 C sifted flour, 1 t ea soda, cinnamon, and nutmeg, 3/4 t salt, and 1 C brown sugar. Mix in 2 C seedless raisins.

Add 1/2 C melted butter to 1 C ea grated carrots, potatoes, and apples. Combine all ingredients and blend well. Turn into well greased pudding mold, cover securely, and steam for 2-1/2 hrs in covered pot of simmering water up about an inch around the mold.

VANILLA SAUCE FOR PLUM PUDDING

Combine 3/4 C sugar, 3 T cornstarch, and 1/4 t ea nutmeg and salt. Add 2 C boiling water in a stream, stirring constantly. Simmer the sauce over low heat, stirring until it is thickened and translucent. Remove from heat, stir in 2 T softened butter a little at a time, and 1-1/2 t vanilla. (2 C)

HARD SAUCE

Cream 3/4 C softened butter with 1 C sifted powdered sugar until smooth with no trace of sugar. Add 1/2 t vanilla or any desired flavoring. Pile lightly on serving dish and sprinkle with nutmeg.

Substitute grated orange rind and/or 2 t orange juice or 2 T rum.

FOAMY SAUCE FOR STEAMED PUDDINGS

Beat 1 egg in top of double boiler, blend in 1 C of sifted powdered sugar, 1/2 C of soft butter, and 1 T vanilla or rum. Keep over hot water until serving time.

RUM PIE

Beat 4 egg yolks until light and lemon-colored, add 2/3 C sugar and 1/4 t salt. In double boiler heat 2 C milk with 1/4 t nutmeg and add to egg mixture, stirring to blend. Return to double boiler and stir until mixture thickens.

Soften 1 envelope unflavored gelatin in 1/4 C water, add to hot mixture, and stir until dissolved. Add 1/3 C rum. Chill until mixture begins to thicken, then fold in 4 egg whites beaten stiff. Spoon into prepared pastry shell and chill. Serve with whipped cream flavored with rum or cover pie with same.

RUM DUM CAKE

Great for New Year's Eve!

Chop 1 C pecans or macadamias and sprinkle evenly in bottom of greased 10 in tube or bundt pan. In bowl, combine 1 package yellow cake mix, 1 package vanilla pudding, 4 eggs, 1/2 C ea rum and water, 1/4 C oil, and blend. Mix for 2 mins at medium speed. Pour batter in prepared pan and bake at 325 for about an hr, or until cake springs back when lightly touched. Cool in pan 15 mins.

Combine 1 C sugar, 1/2 C butter, 1/4 C water and cook, stirring, till it comes to a boil. Stir constantly for 5 mins, then stir in 1/2 - 3/4 C rum, and bring just to the boil. Remove cake to serving plate, prick with pick, and spoon the warm syrup over the warm cake until all is absorbed.

Any leftover eggnog mix? Make **FRENCH TOAST** by dipping slices of white bread in the mixture and frying to a lovely brown on each side in melted butter. Serve with maple syrup.

123

NEW YEAR'S EVE

Ring in the new and ring out the old with a table of hearty pupus and a nourishing soup!

IRENE'S SEVEN LAYER DIP

Spread a 10-1/2 oz can jalapeno bean dip in shallow glass dish. Mash 2 ripe avocados with 1 T lemon juice and spread over beans. Combine 1/4 package taco seasoning, 3 T mayonnaise, and 2 T sour cream, and layer on top of avocado mix. Over this sprinkle 2 oz ea grated Cheddar and Monterey Jack cheese evenly. De-seed and chop 2 ripe tomatoes and place over cheese. Sprinkle 1 C chopped ripe olives over all. Chill well and serve with large corn chips.

CHICKEN LIVER-ONION DIP

Combine 1/4 C water with 2 T dry onion soup mix and set aside.

In small saucepan simmer 1/2 lb chicken livers in water to cover 8-10 mins or till tender, drain, and cool. In blender container combine: onion soup mix, livers, 1 sliced hard-cooked egg, 1/4 C mayonnaise, and 1/2 t Worcestershire sauce. Cover and blend till almost smooth.

Turn into serving bowl and refrigerate. To serve: sprinkle crumbled bacon on top and place in middle of assorted crackers or corn chips.

MATTIE MAJORS' SPINACH SQUARES

Cook and thoroughly drain 1 package frozen chopped spinach.

In a large bowl make a well and mix with a spoon: 1 t baking powder and 1 C flour, 2 slightly beaten eggs and 1 C milk, 1 lb Monterey Jack cheese cut into 1/4 in cubes, and the spinach. Pour into 9x13 in buttered pan and bake in 350 oven for 35 mins. Cool, then cut into 1 in squares. Serve hot or cold.

LOIS HAACK'S ZUCCHINI SQUARES

Mix together thoroughly: 4 C thinly sliced zucchini, 4 slightly beaten eggs, 1/2 C ea finely chopped onion and grated Parmesan, Swiss, or Monterey Jack cheese, and vegetable oil, 1/2 t ea salt, marjoram, and seasoned salt, dash of pepper, 1/8 t garlic powder, 2 T chopped parsley, and 1 C biscuit mix.

Spread in greased 13x9x2 in pan and bake until golden brown, about 30-45 mins. Cool and cut into small pieces.

BETH'S SHRIMP SPREAD

Heat together 1 can tomato soup and 1 8-oz package of cream cheese, add 1 T gelatin, dissolve, and cool.

Add 1/2 C ea finely minced green onions and celery, 1 C mayonnaise, and 1 can shredded shrimp. Mix well, pour into mold, and refrigerate 6-24 hrs, securely covered. Serve with crackers.

Or substitute cream of mushroom soup instead of tomato and combine with crab instead of shrimp. Either way they're delicious.

GORDON'S PROSCIUTTO AND FRUIT

Marinate wedges of any melon in season, pears, or mangoes in port wine. Wrap slices of prosciutto (Italian ham) or plain ham around fruit wedges and secure with cocktail spears. Serve cold garnished with parsley.

HOT CHEDDAR BEAN DIP

Stir the following until well mixed: 1/2 C mayonnaise, 1 16-oz can pinto beans, drained and mashed, 1 C shredded cheddar cheese, 1 4-oz can chopped green chilies, and 1/4 t hot pepper sauce. Spoon into small oven-proof dish and bake in 350 oven 30 mins or till bubbly. Keep warm and serve with chips.

COLD POACHED SALMON

Wrap 1 3-5 lb fresh, cleaned salmon in layers of cheese-cloth.

In poacher or roasting pan with cover combine 4 C water, 2 C dry white wine, 1 sliced onion, 3 stalks celery, sliced, 2 sliced carrots, 1/2 bunch chopped parsley, 1 T black peppercorns, 3 or 4 cloves, 1 t ea salt and dill. Bring to a boil and cover to simmer about half hour.

Gently lower fish into simmering stock and cook over low heat about 35 mins, or 7 mins per lb. Be careful it doesn't boil, just simmers. When fish flakes easily, gently remove from stock and roll onto platter. Unwrap fish, remove skin, cover securely, and chill. Garnish with parsley and slices of lemon sprinkled with paprika.

Serve with **CUCUMBER SAUCE.**

Peel and de-seed 1 large pared cucumber and chop very fine. Let it stand, then drain and squeeze out any liquid. Combine with 1 C sour cream, 1/2 t ea dill and salt, 1-1/2 T vinegar or pickle juice, and dry mustard and sugar to taste.

DORIS ASHE'S PORTUGUESE BEAN SOUP

Soak overnight, drain, and rinse the following: 1/4 package ea small white beans, lentils, large white beans, kidney beans, pinto beans, and split peas.

In a large pot combine beans with following and cook 1-1/2 - 3 hrs: 8 C water, 4 C chicken soup stock, and 1 large ham hock or quarter of a regular ham. Remove ham after cooking, remove bone, fat, and skin, and cut meat in chunks.

Return meat to bean pot and add: 4 stalks celery, 4 carrots, 3 potatoes and 1 large onion all cut in chunks, 1 small shredded cabbage, 1 bay leaf, 1 large can tomatoes, 1 can tomato sauce, 2 Portuguese sausages cut in chunks, and S&P and garlic puree to taste. Simmer 1 hr until vegetables are tender and spices are blended.

INDEX